# THE SCIENCE
# AND PHILOSOPHY
# OF POLITICS

GOVERNANCE: POWER, POLITICS, AND PARTICIPATION

# THE SCIENCE
# AND PHILOSOPHY
# OF POLITICS

EDITED BY BRIAN DUIGNAN, SENIOR EDITOR, RELIGION AND PHILOSOPHY

Britannica®
Educational Publishing

IN ASSOCIATION WITH

ROSEN
EDUCATIONAL SERVICES

Published in 2013 by Britannica Educational Publishing
(a trademark of Encyclopædia Britannica, Inc.)
in association with Rosen Educational Services, LLC
29 East 21st Street, New York, NY 10010.

Distributed exclusively by Rosen Educational Services.
For a listing of additional Britannica Educational Publishing titles, call toll free (800) 237-9932.

First Edition

Britannica Educational Publishing
Adam Augustyn: Assistant Manager
J.E. Luebering: Senior Manager
Marilyn L. Barton: Senior Coordinator, Production Control
Steven Bosco: Director, Editorial Technologies
Lisa S. Braucher: Senior Producer and Data Editor
Yvette Charboneau: Senior Copy Editor
Kathy Nakamura: Manager, Media Acquisition
Brian Duignan, Senior Editor, Religion and Philosophy

Rosen Educational Services
Alexandra Hanson-Harding: Senior Editor
Jeanne Nagle: Editor
Nelson Sá: Art Director
Cindy Reiman: Photography Manager
Brian Garvey: Designer and Cover Design
Introduction by Brian Duignan

**Library of Congress Cataloging-in-Publication Data**

The science and philosophy of politics/edited by Brian Duignan.
    p. cm. — (Governance: power, politics, and participation)
"In association with Britannica Educational Publishing, Rosen Educational Services."
Includes bibliographical references and index.
ISBN 978-1-61530-666-4 (lib. bdg.)
1. Political science. 2. Political science—History. 3. Political science—Philosophy.
4. Political science—Philosophy—History. I. Duignan, Brian.
JA66.S39 2011
320.01—dc23

                                                            2011040135

*Manufactured in the United States of America*

# CONTENTS

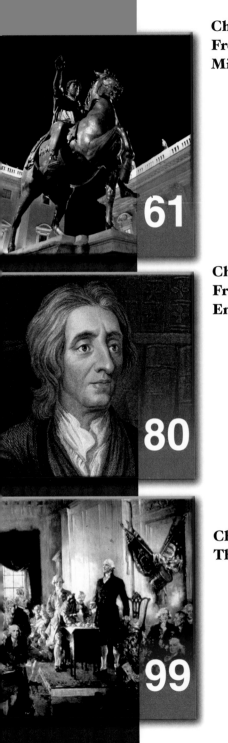

101

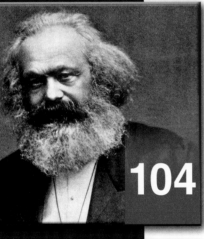

104

129

# INTRODUCTION

The history of political thought in the West begins with the ancient Greeks. During the Classical period of their history (the 5th to the mid-4th century BCE), the Greeks became the first people to study political institutions in a rational, empirical, and systematic way, and the first to think critically about the justification of political authority. In particular, they were the first to conceive of the state as serving a rational purpose, that of enabling its citizens to flourish as human beings. Correlatively, they were the first to recognize human flourishing as necessarily involving some form of participation in political affairs. In

OLLING CENTRE

مركز اقتراع

*Women queue at a polling station in Bentiu, Sudan, waiting to vote in January 2011. The vote was on an independence referendum leading to the partition of Africa's largest nation.* Yasuyoshi Chiba/AFP/Getty Images

part because they conceived of the city-state as the natural form of political organization, their political ideas did not lend themselves naturally to the larger political structures of later European civilizations. Nevertheless, the concepts and vocabulary of Greek political thought served as a framework for the study of politics in subsequent ages, and they continue to inform political scholarship in the present day.

In politics as in many other areas of inquiry, the Greeks did not make a sharp distinction between empirical and strictly philosophical (conceptual and normative) questions. Thus, Aristotle's main work in political philosophy, the *Politics*, is in part an empirically informed analysis of the factors that make for success or failure among city-states. This analysis, in turn, plays a role in his justification of the city-state as the noblest form of human community. Through the rest of the ancient period of European history (until the late 5th century CE), political philosophers occupied themselves with conceptual and normative questions posed by the Greeks as they arose within the new context of empire (the Alexandrian and the Roman) and Christianity, and strictly empirical questions were addressed mainly within the works of historians and biographers. Although many works of political philosophy after the Middle Ages incorporated descriptive observations of varying generality and rigor, it was not until the 19th century that the empirical study of politics was conceived as a distinct discipline, with its own methods and its own basic questions and problems. Political science, as it came to be called, did not supplant political philosophy but instead developed certain areas of inquiry that, for a variety of reasons, had been inadequately explored or not recognized at all.

Modern political science and political philosophy are distinguished by their methods and by their objects of study. Political science (as the term "science" implies) is empirical and descriptive and attempts to explain political institutions and processes as they actually exist on the basis of generalizations drawn from observation, including quantitative measurement. Political philosophy, in contrast, is rationalistic and normative and attempts to analyze fundamental political concepts and values; on that basis it seeks to draw conclusions about what sorts of political arrangements are morally good or logically justified and what sorts are not.

Although they take different approaches, political philosophy and political science are not rivals, and in fact they complement and inform each other. Despite its inherent concern with what ought to be rather than what is, political philosophy must pay attention to the facts of human nature and behavior (such as they are understood) and the general characteristics of human political communities, past and present. If it does not, its analyses and conclusions may become unrealistic and, for that reason, invalid. Thus political philosophy cannot reasonably demand that humans behave in ways that are fundamentally contrary to their nature, and in general no political arrangement can be morally good (much less ideal) for humans unless it is at least possible for humans to achieve.

Political science, on the other hand, must make use of the concepts and values of political philosophy, because they are often built into the very institutions and processes it seeks to explain. Actual political arrangements reflect certain assumptions on the part of those who make them or live in them: assumptions about the proper extent of political authority; the purpose of the state (if any); the relation between the state and other forms of community (such as the family or tribe); the relation between the state and religion; the content of notions such as rights, freedom, justice, self-determination, and self-fulfillment; and the natural qualities and capacities of human beings. Because these assumptions help to explain how certain political institutions come about and how they are sustained, political science must take them into account.

Political science also depends on political philosophy in the sense that much of its research is guided by values and norms that political philosophers have helped to articulate. Studies by political scientists of authoritarian and totalitarian societies, for example, tend to reflect their authors' assumption that such forms of government are unjustified; indeed, much research in this area is undertaken with the explicit goal of understanding, and so forestalling, the conditions that enable authoritarian and totalitarian movements to succeed. Likewise, many studies of bureaucracies and legal systems are motivated by the goal of understanding how effectively such institutions serve the well-being of citizens or protect their political and civil rights.

The first great work of Western political thought is the *Republic* by Plato (*c.* 448-328 BCE). In that dialogue the character Socrates (who in real life was Plato's teacher) seeks to discover what it is for a person to be virtuous, a condition he calls being just or having justice. According to Plato, justice in the individual is not a matter of behaving well but rather of having a soul whose three parts—reason, spirit, and appetite—perform their functions properly and act in harmony for the good of the whole person. The state, too, has three parts, or three social classes: rulers, warriors, and laborers, which are analogous in their functions to the three parts of the soul. Justice in the state, therefore, is a condition in which the three classes perform their functions properly and act in harmony for the good of all citizens.

Plato's most influential student, Aristotle (384-382 BCE), rejected his teacher's utopia as impractical. His largely empirical approach was based on a survey of the constitutions of 158 city-states, which he classified according to the number and purposes of their rulers: a state is ruled either by one person, by a few persons, or by many persons and for the good of everyone or for the good of the ruler(s). In these terms he classified monarchy, aristocracy, and polity as good forms of government and tyranny, oligarchy, and democracy (which he equated with mob rule) as bad ones. According to Aristotle, the purpose of the state is to promote the human good (a life of human flourishing) for all citizens, and the constitution best suited to that goal is polity, which today would be called constitutional democracy.

In the mid-4th century BCE the Greek city-states were subdued by the Macedonian empire of Philip II, whose famous son Alexander the Great vastly extended his father's conquests to the whole of the Mediterranean and eastward to the gates of India. After Alexander's death in 323 BCE, his Mediterranean empire was broken up by his generals into hereditary monarchies; these kingdoms in turn were swept away by the Romans in the second and first centuries BCE. Although city-states continued to exist, they had long since ceased to be independent. Political and ethical philosophy thus adapted themselves to a world in which the Classical political ideal of direct citizen participation no longer applied. The Hellenistic school of Stoicism advocated a kind of ethical self-sufficiency in the face of events beyond one's control, emphasizing individual virtue as the only good, resignation to the divine reason (*logos*) that rules the universe, control of the passions, and faithful adherence to duty. As adapted by Panaetius of Rhodes (*c.* 180-109 BCE) it became popular among the aristocracy of the Roman republic and empire, its most notable adherent being the emperor Marcus Aurelius (ruled 161-180 CE). Stoicism is also important for popularizing the notions of the equal moral worth of all human beings and the existence of a natural moral law that transcends the laws of particular human societies.

The spread of Christianity in the later Roman Empire profoundly affected the development of political philosophy. Early Christian theologians rejected the Classical view that the human good could be achieved in this life through the agency of a wisely run state. In his *City of God*, Augustine of Hippo (354-430 CE) vividly contrasted the Roman institutions of his day with the heavenly kingdom, arguing that the sole concern of humans should be entry into the latter through salvation. For several centuries afterward much Western philosophy was characterized by a cultivated disregard of worldly government as little more than a means of keeping order among a rabble of sinners.

New interest in political philosophy arose in the 12th century with the translation into Latin of the works of Aristotle, which had been almost completely unknown to Western Christian philosophers for 1,000 years. Thomas Aquinas (*c.* 1224-1274) combined Aristotelianism and Christianity, along with themes from Stoicism, in a comprehensive system treating metaphysics, ethics, the philosophy of mind, and political philosophy. Although he favored monarchy, he insisted that rulers are bound by natural moral laws and that the purpose of government is to promote the common good.

In the opinion of many scholars, the first modern political scientist was the Italian diplomat Niccolò Machiavelli (1469-1527). His work *The Prince* consists of advice to current and would-be rulers of Italian city-states about how to gain and hold political power. Because his recommendations included effective but ruthless techniques used by real princes, he was almost immediately condemned as cynical and immoral. The long currency of the term "Machiavellian" reflects his enduring, though undeserved, reputation as an advocate of political evil.

In the 17th century the English philosophers Thomas Hobbes (1588-1679) and John Locke (1632-1704) used the notions of natural law, natural rights, and the social contract (an actual or hypothetical agreement defining the rights and duties of rulers and citizens) to very different ends. Whereas Hobbes defended absolutism, or rule by a monarch with nearly unlimited power, Locke argued for a constitutional division of power between monarch and Parliament and, importantly, for the legitimacy of revolution against a monarch who fails to protect the people's basic rights. In the 18th century the work of Locke and the French philosopher Montesquieu (1689-1755) directly influenced the drafters of the American Declaration of Independence and the U.S. Constitution.

The maturation of natural science in the 17th century, and particularly the spectacular success of Newtonian physics, engendered among philosophers the ambition of constructing analogous "sciences" of human nature and human society. *A Treatise of Human Nature* (1734), by the Scotsman David Hume (1711-1776), was just such an attempt to discover the "secret springs and principles" of human mental life. His investigations, as well as other, more conventional studies, were limited, however, by a lack of sound experimental methods and reliable sources of data. This situation began to change in the early 19th century, when Henri de Saint-Simon and Auguste Comte laid the conceptual foundation for what they hoped would be a "positive" science of society. Although their vision never yielded a grand overarching discipline, it did eventually lead to the separate development of economics, sociology, psychology, and political science. Academic departments and schools of political science were first established in western Europe and the United States in the late 19th century.

The work of Karl Marx (1818-1883) and Friedrich Engels (1820-1895) straddled the newly established divide between political philosophy, political science, and economics. They combined a theory of the state as an instrument of class domination (by those who own the means of production) with a materialist philosophy of history adapted from the dialectical metaphysics of G.W.F. Hegel (1770-1827). Although the great proletarian revolution they claimed was inevitable never really occurred (at least not as they imagined it), their ideas became the basis of the communist ideologies of the 20th century as well as of western European democratic socialism. Since the 1930s Marxist schools of thought have flourished in several areas of philosophy as well as in political science, economics, and other social sciences.

By the turn of the 20th century the institutional as well as conceptual separation of political science and political philosophy was complete. The range of phenomena investigated by political science and the sophistication of its conceptual and empirical methods have grown enormously since then, so much so that it has spawned several new subfields dealing with areas such as comparative politics, democratic theory, public administration and law, and international relations. Developments in political philosophy, meanwhile, have included the transformation of Lockean political liberalism into a sophisticated theory of justice, a countervailing movement to ground a theory of justice in the notion of natural rights, and, significantly, a revival of interest in the ethics and politics of Aristotle. Throughout this period political science and political philosophy have continued to guide and inform each other as they have, in their different ways, deepened our understanding of politics. Readers are invited to deepen their own understanding through the pages of this book.

# CHAPTER 1

## The Study of Politics: Scientific and Philosophical Approaches

Politics, the art or craft of governance, has been a central topic of philosophical speculation in the West since the time of the ancient Greeks. Beginning with Plato and especially Aristotle, political philosophers examined abstract political ideas and values, such as rights, justice, freedom, and political obligation and authority, and constructed theories of the proper powers, functions, and organization of the state.

These political philosophers' general approach was normative, or concerned with standards, rather than descriptive. In other words, they were concerned with what ought to be rather than with what is. Their methods were rationalistic (emphasizing reason) and speculative (theoretical rather than demonstrable), though some philosophers, notably Aristotle, produced valuable descriptive studies of the political systems and institutions of their day.

Politics was not studied as a science in the modern sense of the term until the 19th century, when aspects of human behaviour and social life that until then had been investigated by political philosophers, philosophers of history, and philosophers of mind came to be conceived as coherent fields of inquiry within a broad new "science of society." During the course of the century a number of distinct social sciences were recognized, including political

PLATO FLORVIT OLYMP 98.
*Magnus Aristoteles maior Plato noueratile*
*Naturam rerum, noucrat iste Deum.*

*The ancient Greek philosopher Plato.*
Hulton Archive/Getty Images

science, sociology, economics, psychology, and cultural anthropology. Political science, like the other new fields, did not replace the branch of philosophy from which it had emerged but rather adopted a new approach and set of methodologies, along with a new range of problems. In contrast to political philosophy, political science is descriptive rather than normative, and empirical (based on experience) rather than speculative. It studies existing political institutions and behaviour and attempts to develop explanatory theories or other generalizations based on empirical observations, which it expresses in quantitative terms where possible.

## THE NATURE AND SCOPE OF POLITICAL SCIENCE

Political science may be defined as the systematic study of governance by the application of scientific methods of analysis. As traditionally understood, it examines the state and its organs and institutions. The contemporary discipline, however, is considerably broader than this, encompassing studies of all the societal, cultural, and psychological factors that mutually influence the operation of government and the body politic. Although political science borrows heavily from the other social sciences, it is distinguished from them by its focus on power—defined as the ability of one political actor to get another actor to do what it wants—at the international, national, and local levels.

Political science, like all modern sciences, involves empirical investigation—i.e.; originating in or based on observation or experience. But it generally does not produce precise measurements and predictions. This has led some scholars to question whether the discipline can be accurately described as a science. However, if the term *science* applies to any body of systematically organized knowledge based on facts ascertained by empirical methods and described by as much measurement as the material allows, then political science is a science, like the other social disciplines. In the 1960s the American historian and philosopher of science Thomas S. Kuhn argued that political science was "pre-paradigmatic," not yet having developed basic research paradigms, such as the periodic table that defines chemistry. It is likely that political science never will develop a single, universal paradigm or theory, and attempts to do so have seldom lasted more than a generation, making political science a discipline of many trends but few classics.

Modern political science is conventionally divided into several fields, each of which contains various subfields.

1. Domestic politics is generally the most common field of study. Its subfields include public opinion, elections, national government, and state, local, or regional government.
2. Comparative politics focuses on politics within countries (often grouped into world regions) and analyzes similarities and differences between countries.

3

3. International relations considers the political relationships and interactions between countries, including the causes of war, the formation of foreign policy, international political economy (the study of interactions between political and economic institutions at the international level), and the structures that increase or decrease the policy options available to governments.

4. Political theory includes classical as well as contemporary political philosophy and other general theories of politics.

5. Public administration studies the role of the bureaucracy. It is the field most oriented toward practical applications within political science and is often organized as a separate department that prepares students for careers in the civil service.

6. Public law studies constitutions, legal systems, civil rights, and criminal justice (now increasingly its own discipline).

7. Public policy examines the passage and implementation of all types of government policies, particularly those related to civil rights, defense, health, education, economic growth, urban renewal, regional development, and environmental protection.

# SOCIAL SCIENCE

"Social science" is a term that applies to any discipline or branch of science that deals with human behaviour in its social and cultural aspects. The social sciences include cultural (or social) anthropology, sociology, social psychology, political science, and economics. Also frequently included are social and economic geography and those areas of education that deal with the social contexts of learning and the relation of the school to the social order. History is regarded by many as a social science, and certain areas of historical study are almost indistinguishable from work done in the social sciences. Most historians, however, consider history as one of the humanities. It is generally best, in any case, to consider history as marginal to the humanities and social sciences, since its insights and techniques pervade both. The study of comparative law may also be regarded as a part of the social sciences, although it is ordinarily pursued in schools of law rather than in departments or schools containing most of the other social sciences.

Although, strictly speaking, the social sciences do not precede the 19th century—that is, as distinct and recognized disciplines of thought—one must go back further in time for the origins of some of their fundamental ideas and objectives. In the largest sense, the origins go all the way back to the ancient Greeks and their rationalist inquiries into the nature of humans, state, and morality. The heritage of both Greece and Rome is a powerful one in the history of social thought as it is in other areas of Western society. Very probably, apart from the initial Greek determination to study all things in the spirit of dispassionate and rational inquiry, there would be no social sciences today.

## THE NATURE AND SCOPE OF POLITICAL PHILOSOPHY

Political philosophy is the branch of philosophy that is concerned, at the most abstract level, with the concepts and arguments involved in political opinion. The meaning of the term *political* is itself one of the major problems of political philosophy. Broadly, however, one may characterize as political all those practices and institutions that are concerned with government. In this volume, some of the important figures you will be reading about played important roles in the development of both political science and political philosophy.

The central problem of political philosophy is how to deploy or limit public power so as to maintain the survival and enhance the quality of human life. Like all aspects of human experience, political philosophy is conditioned by environment and by the scope and limitations of mind, and the answers given by successive political philosophers to perennial problems reflect the knowledge and the assumptions of their times. Political philosophy is inevitably related to general philosophy and is itself a subject of cultural anthropology, sociology, and the sociology of knowledge. As a normative discipline it is thus concerned with what ought, on various assumptions, to be and how this purpose can be promoted, rather than with a description of facts—although any realistic political theory is necessarily related to these facts.

*View of the House Chamber as U.S. Pres. Barack Obama delivers the annual State of the Union address at the Capitol in Washington, DC, in January 2011. Nicholas Kamm/AFP/Getty Images*

Political philosophy is not merely unpractical speculation. It has had decisive results on political action, for the assumptions on which political life is conducted clearly must influence what actually happens. Political philosophy may thus be viewed as one of the most important intellectual disciplines, for it sets standards of judgment and defines constructive purposes for the use of public power. Such consideration of the purposes for which power should be used is in a sense even more urgent today than it was in earlier periods, for humankind has at its disposal the power either to create a world civilization in which modern technology can benefit the human race or to extinguish itself through war or by destroying the natural environment on which human life depends. The scope for political philosophy is thus great, the clarification of its purpose and limitations urgent—an aspect, indeed, of civilization's survival.

Despite this unique aspect of the contemporary situation, and although ancient political philosophies were formulated under very different conditions, their study still illuminates vital questions today. Questions concerning the aims of government, the grounds of political obligation, the rights of individuals against the state, the basis of sovereignty, and the nature of political liberty and social justice have been asked and answered in many ways over the centuries. They are all fundamental to political philosophy and demand answers in terms of modern knowledge and opinion.

# CHAPTER 2

## Political Science: From Antiquity to the Early 20th Century

A lthough political science is an inherently modern discipline, it has historical antecedents dating to ancient times. Analyses of politics appeared in ancient cultures in works by various thinkers, including China's Confucius (551–479 BCE). Writings by the historian Ibn Khaldūn (1332–1406) in North Africa have greatly influenced the study of politics in the Arabic-speaking world. But the fullest explication of politics has been in the West. Some have identified Plato (428/427–348/347 BCE), whose ideal of a stable republic still yields insights and metaphors, as the first political scientist, though most consider Aristotle (384–322 BCE), to be the discipline's true founder.

### ARISTOTLE AND THE STOICS

Aristotle's students gathered descriptions of 158 Greek city-states (a city-state is called a polis), which Aristotle used to formulate his famous sixfold typology of political systems. He distinguished political systems by the number of persons ruling (one, few, or many) and by whether the form was legitimate (rulers governing in the interests of all) or corrupt (rulers governing in their own interests). Legitimate systems included monarchy (rule by one), aristocracy (rule by the few), and polity (rule by the many), while corresponding corrupt forms were tyranny (corrupt rule by one); oligarchy (corrupt rule by a minority), and

8

democracy (anarchy or mob rule). Aristotle considered democracy to be the worst form of government, though in his classification it meant mob rule. The best form of government, a polity, was, in contemporary terms, akin to an efficient, stable democracy. Aristotle presciently noted that a polity functions best if the middle class is large, a point confirmed by modern empirical findings. Aristotle's classification endured for centuries and is still helpful in understanding political systems.

Plato and Aristotle focused on perfecting the polis, a tiny political entity, which for the Greeks meant both society and political system. The conquest of the Mediterranean world and beyond by Aristotle's pupil Alexander the Great (336–323 BCE) and, after his death, the division of Alexander's empire among his generals brought large new political forms to the Greek world, in which society and political system came to be seen as separate entities. This shift required a new understanding of politics. Hellenistic thinkers, especially the Stoics, asserted the existence of a natural law that applied to all human beings equally; this idea became the foundation of Roman legalism and Christian notions of equality. Thus, the Roman orator Marcus Tullius Cicero (106–43 BCE), who was strongly influenced by the Stoics, was noteworthy for his belief that all human beings, regardless of their wealth or citizenship, possessed an equal moral worth.

## EARLY CHRISTIAN AND MEDIEVAL THINKERS

Early Christian thinkers, such as St. Augustine (354–430), emphasized the dual loyalty of Christians to both God and temporal (earthly) rulers, with the clear implication that the "heavenly city" is more important and durable than the earthly one. With this came an otherworldly disdain for politics. For eight centuries knowledge of Aristotle was lost to Europe but preserved by Arab philosophers such as al-Fārābiī (*c.* 878–*c.* 950) and Averroës (1126–1198). Latin translations of Aristotle revitalized European thought after about 1200. St. Thomas Aquinas (1224/25–1274) Christianized Aristotle's *Politics* to lend it moral purpose. Aquinas took from Aristotle the idea that humans are both rational and social, that states occur naturally, and that government can improve humans spiritually. Thus, Aquinas favoured monarchy but despised tyranny, arguing that kingly authority should be limited by law and used for the common good. The philosopher Marsilius of Padua (*c.* 1280–*c.* 1343), in *Defensor Pacis* (1324; "Defender of the Peace"), introduced secularization by elevating the state over the church as the originator of laws. For this, as well as for proposing that legislators be elected, Marsilius ranks as an important modernizer.

## EARLY MODERN DEVELOPMENTS

Although the field of political science did not formally emerge until the 19th century, as discussed earlier, the field had its forefathers. The first of these could be considered the Florentine writer Niccolò Machiavelli (1469–1527).

His infamous work *The Prince* (1531), a treatise originally dedicated to Florence's ruler, Lorenzo di Piero de' Medici, presented amoral advice to actual and would-be princes on the best means of acquiring and holding on to political power. Machiavelli's political philosophy, which completed the secularization of politics begun by Marsilius, was based on reason rather than religion. An early Italian patriot, Machiavelli believed that Italy could be unified and its foreign occupiers expelled only by ruthless and single-minded princes who rejected any moral constraints on their power.

Machiavelli introduced the modern idea of power—how to get it and how to use it—as the crux of politics, a viewpoint shared by some contemporary schools of international relations, including "realism," rational choice theory, and others. Machiavelli thus ranks alongside Aristotle as a founder of political science.

The English philosopher Thomas Hobbes (1588–1679) also placed power at the centre of his political analysis. In

_Niccolò Machiavelli._ Hulton Archive/ Getty Images

_Leviathan; or, The Matter, Form, and Power of a Commonwealth, Ecclesiastical and Civil_ (1651), completed near the end of the English Civil Wars (1642–51), Hobbes outlined, without reference to an all-powerful God, how humans, endowed with a natural right to self-preservation but living in an anarchic state of nature, would be driven by fear of violent death to form a civil society and submit to a single sovereign authority (a monarch) to ensure their peace and security through a social contract—an actual or hypothetical agreement between citizens and their rulers that defines the rights and duties of each. The English philosopher John Locke (1632–1704), who also witnessed the turmoil of an English civil war—the Glorious Revolution (1688–89)—argued in his influential _Two Treatises of Government_ (1689) that people form governments through a social contract to preserve their inalienable natural rights to "life, liberty, and property." He further maintained that any government that fails to secure the natural rights of its citizens may properly be overthrown. Locke's views were a powerful force in the intellectual life of 18th-century colonial America and constituted the philosophical basis of the American Declaration of Independence (1776), many of whose drafters, particularly Thomas Jefferson (1743–1826), were well acquainted with Locke's writings.

If Hobbes was the conservative of the "contractualists" and Locke the liberal, then the French philosopher Jean-Jacques Rousseau (1712–78) was the radical. Rousseau's *The Social Contract* (1762) constructs a civil society in which the separate wills of individuals are combined to govern as the "general will" (*volonté générale*) of the collective that overrides individual wills, "forcing a man to be free." Rousseau's radical vision was embraced by French revolutionaries and later by totalitarians, who distorted many of his philosophical lessons.

Montesquieu (1689–1755), a more pragmatic French philosopher, contributed to modern comparative politics with his *The Spirit of Laws* (1748). Montesquieu's sojourn in England convinced him that English liberties were based on the separation and balance of power between Parliament and the monarchy, a principle later embraced by the framers of the Constitution of the United States. Montesquieu also produced an innovative analysis of governance that assigned to each form of government an animating principle—for example, republics are based on virtue, monarchies on honour, and despotisms on fear. Montesquieu's analysis concluded that a country's form of government is determined not by the locus of political power but by how the government enacts public policy.

The Scottish economist and philosopher Adam Smith (1723–90) is considered the founder of classical economic liberalism. In *An Inquiry into the Nature and Causes of the*

*Wealth of Nations* (1776), he argued that the role of the state should be restricted primarily to enforcing contracts in a free market. In contrast, the classical conservatism of the English parliamentarian Edmund Burke (1729–1797) maintained that established values and institutions were essential elements of all societies and that revolutions that sought to destroy such values (e.g., the French Revolution) delivered people to irrational impulses and to tyranny. Burke thus introduced an important psychological or cultural insight: that political systems are living organisms that grow over centuries and that depend on a sense of legitimacy that is gradually built up among their subjects.

The early development of political science was also influenced by law. The French political philosopher Jean Bodin (1530–1596) articulated a theory of sovereignty that viewed the state as the ultimate source of law in a given territory. Bodin's work, which was undertaken as the modern state was first developing, provided a justification of the legitimacy of national governments, one fiercely defended to this day. Many political scientists, especially in international relations, find Bodin's notion of sovereignty useful for expressing the legitimacy and equality of states.

## SEPARATION OF POWERS

Separation of powers is the division of the legislative, executive, and judicial functions of government among separate and independent bodies. Such a separation, it has been argued, limits the possibility of arbitrary excesses by government, since the sanction of all three branches is required for the making, executing, and administering of laws.

The doctrine may be traced to ancient and medieval theories of mixed government, which argued that the processes of government should involve the different elements in society such as monarchic, aristocratic, and democratic interests. The first modern formulation of the doctrine was that of Montesquieu in *De l'esprit des lois* (1748), although Locke had earlier argued that legislative power should be divided between king and Parliament.

Montesquieu's argument that liberty is most effectively safeguarded by the separation of powers was inspired by the English constitution, although his interpretation of English political realities has since been disputed. His work was widely influential, most notably in America, where it profoundly influenced the framing of the Constitution. The U.S. Constitution further precluded the concentration of political power by providing staggered terms of office in the key governmental bodies.

Modern constitutional systems show a great variety of arrangements of the legislative, executive, and judicial processes, and the doctrine has consequently lost much of its rigidity and dogmatic purity. In the 20th and 21st centuries, and especially since World War II, governmental involvement in numerous aspects of social and economic life has resulted in an enlargement of the scope of executive power. Some who fear the consequences of this for individual liberty have favoured establishing means of appeal against executive and administrative decisions (for example, through an ombudsman), rather than attempting to reassert the doctrine of the separation of powers.

## THE 19TH CENTURY

Contemporary political science traces its roots primarily to the 19th century, when the rapid growth of the natural sciences stimulated enthusiasm for the creation of a new social science. Capturing this fervour of scientific optimism was Antoine-Louis-Claude, Comte Destutt de Tracy (1754–1836), who in the 1790s coined the term *idéologie* ("ideology") for his "science of ideas," which, he believed, could perfect society. Also pivotal to the empirical movement was the French utopian socialist Henri de

Saint-Simon (1760–1825), a founder of Christian socialism, who in 1813 suggested that morals and politics could
become "positive" sciences—that is, disciplines whose
authority would rest not upon subjective preconceptions
but upon objective evidence. Saint-Simon collaborated
with the French mathematician and philosopher Auguste
Comte (1798–1857), considered by many to be the founder
of sociology, on the publication of the *Plan of the Scientific
Operations Necessary for the Reorganization of Society* (1822),
which claimed that politics would become a social physics
and discover scientific laws of social progress. Although
"Comtean positivism," with its enthusiasm for the scientific study of society and its emphasis on using the results
of such studies for social improvement, is still very much
alive in psychology, contemporary political science shows
only traces of Comte's optimism.

The scientific approach to politics developed during
the 19th century along two distinct lines that still divide
the discipline. In the 1830s the French historian and
politician Alexis de Tocqueville (1805–59) brilliantly ana-
lyzed democracy in America, concluding that it worked
because Americans had developed "the art of association" and were egalitarian group formers. Tocqueville's
emphasis on cultural values contrasted sharply with the
views of the German socialist theorists Karl Marx (1818–
1883) and Friedrich Engels (1820–1895), who advanced
a materialistic and economic theory of the state as an
instrument of domination by the classes that own the
means of production. According to Marx and Engels,
prevailing values and culture simply reflect the tastes and
needs of ruling elites; the state, they charged, is merely
"the steering committee of the bourgeoisie." Asserting
what they considered to be an immutable scientific law
of history, they argued that the state would soon be overthrown by the industrial working class (the proletariat),

who would institute socialism, a just and egalitarian form of governance.

The first separate school of political science was established in 1872 in France as the École Libre des Sciences Politiques (now the Institut d'Études Politiques). In 1895 the London School of Economics and Political Science was founded in England, and the first chair of politics was established at the University of Oxford in 1912.

## THE EARLY 20TH CENTURY: DEVELOPMENTS IN THE UNITED STATES

Some of the most important developments in political science since it became a distinct academic discipline have occurred in the United States. Politics had long been studied in American universities, but usually as part of the curricula of law, philosophy, or economics. Political science as a separate discipline in universities in the United States dates from 1880, when John W. Burgess, after studying at the École Libre in Paris, established a school of political science at Columbia University in New York City. Although political science faculties grew unevenly after 1900, by the 1920s most major institutions had established new departments, variously named political science, government, or politics.

Political science in the United States in the last quarter of the 19th century was influenced by the experience of numerous scholars who had done graduate work at German universities, where the discipline was taught as *Staatswissenschaft* ("science of the state") in an ordered, structured, and analytic organization of concepts, definitions, comparisons, and inferences. This highly formalistic and institutional approach, which focused on constitutions, dominated American political science until World War II. The work of American political scientists represented an effort to establish an autonomous discipline, separate from history, moral philosophy, and political economy. Among the new scholars were Woodrow Wilson (1856–1924), who would be elected president of the United States in 1912, and Frank Goodnow (1859-1939), a Columbia University professor of administrative law and, later, president of Johns Hopkins University, who was among the first to study municipal governments. Their writing showed an awareness of new intellectual currents, such as the theory of evolution. Inspired by the work of Charles Darwin (1809–82), Wilson and others led a transformation of American political science from the study of static institutions to the study of social facts, more truly in the positivist temper, less in the analytic tradition, and more oriented toward realism.

Pres. Woodrow Wilson (standing, right) being cheered as he passes through the streets of San Francisco, Calif., in 1915. Wilson was an influential political science scholar in the late 1800s and early 1900s. Hirz/Archive Photos/Getty Images

Arthur F. Bentley's *The Process of Government*, little noticed at the time of its publication in 1908, greatly influenced the development of political science from the 1930s to the 1950s. Bentley (1870-1957) rejected statist abstractions in favour of observable facts and identified groups and their interactions as the basis of political life. Group activity, he argued, determined legislation, administration, and adjudication. In emphasizing behaviour and process, Bentley sounded themes that later became central to political science. In particular, his insistence that "all social movements are brought about by group interaction" is the defining feature of contemporary pluralist and interest-group approaches.

Although Bentley's effort to develop an objective, value-free analysis of politics had no initial consequence, other movements toward this goal enjoyed more immediate success. The principal impetus came from the University of Chicago, where what became known as the Chicago school developed in the mid-1920s and thereafter. The leading figure in this movement was Charles E. Merriam, whose *New Aspects of Politics* (1925) argued for a reconstruction of method in political analysis, urged the greater use of statistics in the aid of empirical observation and measurement, and postulated that "intelligent social control"—a concept reminiscent of the old Comtean positivism—might emerge from the converging interests of politics, medicine, psychiatry, and psychology. Because Merriam's basic political datum at this stage was "attitude," he relied largely on the insights of psychology for a better understanding of politics. An important empirical work of the Chicago school was Merriam and Harold F. Gosnell's *Non-voting, Causes and Methods of Control* (1924), which used sampling methods and survey data and is illustrative of the type of research that came to dominate political science after World War II. Merriam's approach was not entirely new; in 1908 the British political scientist Graham Wallas (1858–1932) had argued in *Human Nature in Politics* that a new political science should favour the quantification of psychological elements (human nature), including nonrational and subconscious inferences, a view similarly expressed in *Public Opinion* (1922) by the American journalist and political scientist Walter Lippmann (1889–1974).

Harold Lasswell (1902–1978), a member of the Chicago group, carried the psychological approach to Yale University, where he had a commanding influence. His *Psychopathology and Politics* (1930) and *Power and Personality* (1948) fused categories of Freudian psychology with considerations of power. Many political scientists attempted to use Freudian psychology to analyze politics, but none succeeded in establishing it as a firm basis of political science, because it depended too much on subjective insights and often could not be verified empirically. Lasswell, for example, viewed politicians as unbalanced people with an inordinate need for power, whereas "normal" people had no compulsion for political office. Although intuitively insightful, this notion is difficult—if not impossible—to prove scientifically.

Merriam's *Political Power* (1934) and Lasswell's classic *Politics: Who Gets What, When, How* (1936)—the title of which articulated the basic definition of politics—gave a central place to the phenomenon of power in the study of politics. Merriam discussed how power comes into being, how it becomes "authority" (which he equated with power), the techniques of power holders, the defenses of those over whom power is wielded, and the dissipation of power. Lasswell focused on "influence and the influential," laying the basis for subsequent "elite" theories of politics. Although the various members of the Chicago school ostensibly sought to develop political science as a value-free discipline, it had two central predilections: it accepted democratic values, and it attempted to improve the operation of democratic systems. Power approaches also became central in the burgeoning field of international relations, particularly after World War II. Hans Morgenthau (1904–1980), a German refugee and analyst of world politics, argued succinctly in *Politics Among Nations* (1948) that "all politics is a struggle for power."

The totalitarian dictatorships that developed in Europe and Asia in the 1920s and '30s and the onset of World War II turned political science, particularly in the United States, away from its focus on institutions, law, and procedures. The constitution of Germany's post–World War I Weimar Republic had been an excellent model, but it failed in practice because too few Germans were then committed supporters of democracy. Likewise, the Soviet Union's 1936 constitution appeared democratic but in reality was merely an attempt to mask the brutal dictatorship of Joseph Stalin. Works of this period focused on the role of elites, political parties, and interest groups, on legislative and bureaucratic processes, and especially on how voters in democracies make their electoral choices. This new interest in actual political behaviour became known as "behavioralism," a term borrowed from psychology's behaviourism. Whereas most earlier thinkers had focused on the "top" of the political system—its institutions—behavioralists instead explored the "bottom," especially that which could be quantified. The result was that much of political science became political sociology.

## THE EARLY 20TH CENTURY: DEVELOPMENTS OUTSIDE THE UNITED STATES

Since the time of Marx and Engels, political scientists have continued to debate the relative importance of culture and economic structures in determining human behaviour and the organization of society. In the late 19th and early 20th centuries, the Italian economists Gaetano Mosca (1858–1941) and Vilfredo Pareto (1848–1923) echoed Marx's analysis that society was ruled by elites, but they considered this both permanent and natural. They were joined by the German-born Italian political sociologist and economist Robert Michels (1876–1936), whose "iron law of oligarchy" declared rule by the few to be inevitable. Mosca, Pareto, and Michels all agreed that the overthrow of the existing "political class" would simply result in its replacement by another, a view that was supported in the mid-20th century by Yugoslav dissident Milovan Djilas (1911–1995) in his *The New Class* (1957). Pareto also contributed the idea (which he borrowed from economics) that society is a system tending toward equilibrium: like an economic system, a society that becomes out of balance will tend to correct itself by developing new institutions and laws or by redistributing power. This approach was adopted by much of academic political science after World War II and was later developed by "systems" theory.

In the early 20th century, the Swedish political scientist Rudolf Kjellén (1864–1922) treated the state as a fusion of organic and cultural elements determined by geography. Kjellén is credited with coining the term *geopolitics* (*geopolitik*), which acquired a sinister connotation in the years after World War I, when German expansionists appealed to geopolitical arguments in support of the Nazi regime of Adolf Hitler. Although geopolitics still exerts a considerable influence on political science, particularly in the areas of international relations and foreign policy, the discipline of political geography developed into a distinct subfield of geography rather than of political science.

The German sociologist Max Weber (1864–1920), who rejected Marx and embraced Tocqueville's emphasis on culture and values, was perhaps the most influential figure in political science in the late 19th and early 20th centuries. Marx had proposed that capitalism gave rise to Protestantism: the merchants and princes of northern Europe developed commerce to such an extent that Roman Catholic restrictions had to be discarded. Weber rejected this idea, claiming that Protestantism triggered capitalism: the Calvinist idea of predestination led individuals to try to prove, by amassing capital, that they were predestined for heaven. Weber's theory of the Protestant ethic is still disputed, but not the fact that religion and culture powerfully influence economic and political development.

Weber understood that the social sciences could not simply mimic the natural sciences, because humans attach widely varying meanings and loyalties to their leaders and institutions. It is not simply facts that matter but how people perceive, interpret, and react to these facts; this makes causality in the social sciences far more complex than in the natural sciences. To be objective, therefore, the social scientist must take into account human subjectivity.

Weber discerned three types of authority: traditional (as in monarchies), charismatic (a concept he developed to refer to the personal drawing power of revolutionary leaders), and rational-legal (characteristic of modern societies). Weber coined the term *bureaucracy*, and he was the first to study bureaucracies systematically. His theories, which focused on culture as a chief source of economic growth and democracy, still find support among contemporary political scientists, and he must be ranked equally as one of the founders of both modern sociology and modern political science.

*German sociologist Max Weber, who championed objectivity in social science and analysis of the motives behind human action.* Hulton Archive/Getty Images

Other scholars also contributed to the growth of political science in the 19th and early 20th centuries. In *The English Constitution* (1867), the English economist and political analyst Walter Bagehot (1826–1877), who was also an editor of *The Economist*, famously distinguished between Britain's "dignified" offices (e.g., the monarch) and its "efficient" offices (e.g., the prime minister). James Bryce (1838–1922), who taught civil law at the University of Oxford, produced one of the earliest and most influential studies of the U.S. political system in *The American Commonwealth* (1888). The Belorussian political scientist Moisey Ostrogorsky (1854–1919), who was educated at the École Libre des Sciences Politiques in Paris, pioneered the study of parties, elections, and public opinion in *Democracy and the Organization of Political Parties* (originally written in French; 1902), which focused on the United States and Britain. In Paris, André Siegfried, teaching at the École Libre des Sciences Politiques and the Collège de France, introduced the use of maps to demonstrate the influence of geography on politics. At first few Britons turned to behavioralism and quantification, instead continuing in their inclination toward political philosophy. In contrast, the Swedish scholar Herbert Tingsten (1896–1973), in his seminal *Political Behaviour: Studies in Election Statistics* (1937), developed the connections between social groups and their voting tendencies. Before World War II the large areas of the world that were colonies or dictatorships made few important contributions to the growth of political science.

# CHAPTER 3

## Political Science: From the Mid-20th Century to the Present

Perhaps the most important irreversible change in political science after World War II was that the scope of the discipline was expanded to include the study of politics in Asia, Africa, and Latin America—areas that had been largely ignored in favour of Europe and North America. This trend was encouraged by the Cold War competition between the United States and the Soviet Union for influence over the political development of newly independent countries. The scholarship produced in these countries, however, remained largely derivative of developments in Europe and the United States. Researchers in Asia, Africa, and Latin America, often in partnership with European and American colleagues, produced significant studies on decolonization, ideology, federalism, corruption, and political instability. In Latin America, a Marxist-oriented view called "dependency theory" was popular from the 1960s to the '80s. Greatly influencing the study of international relations in the United States and Europe as well as in developing countries, dependency theorists argued that Latin America's problems were rooted in its subservient economic and political relationship to the United States and western Europe. More recently, Latin American political scientists, influenced by methods developed in American universities, undertook empirical studies of the sources of democracy and instability, such as Arturo Valenzuela's *The Breakdown of Democratic Regimes* (1978). African, Asian, and Latin American political scientists also made important contributions as teachers on the faculties of American and European universities.

Outside the United States, where political science initially was less quantitative, there were several outstanding works. Like Lasswell, the German philosopher Theodor Adorno (1903–1969) and others adopted Freudian insights in their pioneering study *The Authoritarian Personality* (1950), which used a 29-item questionnaire to detect the susceptibility of individuals to fascist beliefs. The French political scientist Maurice Duverger's *Political Parties* (1951) is still highly regarded, not only for its classification of parties but also for its linking of party systems with electoral systems. Duverger argued that single-member-district electoral systems that require only a plurality to win election tend to produce two-party systems, whereas proportional-representation systems tend to produce multiparty systems; this generalization was later called "Duverger's law." The French sociologist Michel Crozier's *The Bureaucratic Phenomenon* (1964) found that Weber's idealized bureaucracy is quite messy, political, and varied. Each bureaucracy is a political subculture; what is rational and routine in one bureau may be quite different in another. Crozier thus influenced the subsequent "bureaucratic politics" approach of the 1970s.

## BEHAVIORALISM

Behavioralism, which was one of the dominant approaches in the 1950s and '60s, is the view that the subject matter of political science should be limited to phenomena that are independently observable and quantifiable. It assumes that political institutions largely reflect underlying social forces and that the study of politics should begin with society, culture, and public opinion. To this end, behavioralists utilize the methodology of the social sciences—primarily psychology—to establish statistical relationships between independent variables (presumed causes) and dependent variables (presumed effects). For example, a behavioralist might use detailed election data to argue that voters in rural areas tend to vote for candidates who are more conservative, while voters in cities generally favour candidates who are more liberal. The prominence of behavioralists in the post-World War II period helped to lead political science in a much more scientific direction. For many behavioralists, only such quantified studies can be considered political science in the strict sense; they often contrasted their studies with those of the so-called traditionalists, who attempted to explain politics by using unquantified descriptions, anecdotes, historical analogies, ideologies, and philosophy. Like behaviourism in psychology, behavioralism in political science attempted to discard intuition, or at least to support it with empirical observation. A traditionalist, in contrast, might attempt to support intuition with reason alone.

Perhaps the most important behavioral contributions to political science were election studies. In 1955 American political scientist V.O. Key, Jr. (1908–63), identified as "critical," or "realigning," several elections in which American voters shifted their long-term party affiliation massively from one political party to another, giving rise to the dominance of the Republican Party from 1860 to 1932 and of the Democratic Party after 1932. Pioneering statistical electoral analyses were conducted by the University of Michigan's Survey Research Center (SRC), which was developed in the 1940s. In *The American Voter* (1960), Angus Campbell, Philip Converse, William Miller, and Donald Stokes used the results of studies by the SRC to develop the concept of party identification—the long-term psychological attachment of a voter to a political party. The long-recognized influences of religion, social class, region, and ethnicity, they argued, contribute to voting behaviour only insofar as the voter has been socialized, primarily by his parents, to adopt a particular party identification.

Behavioral approaches were soon adopted outside the United States, often by scholars with connections to American universities. The University of Oxford initiated election studies in the 1960s, and David Butler and Donald Stokes—one of the authors of *The American Voter*—adapted much of the American study in *Political Change in Britain: Forces Shaping Electoral Choice* (1969). They found that political generation (the era in which one was born) and "duration of partisanship" also predict party identification—that is, the length of time one has been a partisan heavily predicts one's vote. They also found that party identification, initially transmitted by one's parents, may change under the impact of historic events. The influential Norwegian scholar Stein Rokkan pioneered the use of cross-national quantitative data to examine the interaction of party systems and social divisions based on class, religion, and region, which in combination explain much voting behaviour. Rokkan identified the importance of "centre-periphery" tensions, finding that outlying regions of a country tend to vote differently from the area where political and economic activities are centred.

The extensive Eurobarometer series—public-opinion surveys carried out in European Union countries since 1973 on behalf of the European Commission—have given European behavioralists a solid statistical base on a range of political, social, economic, and cultural issues; the surveys have provided valuable data for examining trends over time, and they have shown, among other things, that modern European ideological opinion clusters around the political centre, suggesting that stable democratic systems have taken root. More recently, Transparency International, founded in 1993 in Berlin, has conducted worldwide surveys that attempt to quantify corruption. In Latin America, Guillermo O'Donnell and Arturo Valenzuela used public-opinion surveys and voting, economic, and demographic data to examine the forces that have destabilized democracy there.

European Union officials Michel Platini (right) and Androulla Vassilliou holding a press conference in March 2010 announcing a Eurobarometer survey on sport at EU headquarters in Brussels, Belgium. Georges Gobet/AFP/Getty Images

The behavioral approach was also central to the work of the American sociologist and political scientist Seymour Martin Lipset, whose influential *Political Man: The Social Bases of Politics* (1960) used statistical and historical data to demonstrate that social class is one of the chief determinants of political behaviour. Lipset infuriated Marxists by portraying elections as "the democratic class struggle" in which the working class finds its true voice in moderate leftist parties. Lipset also contributed to modernization theory by identifying factors that explain why countries adopt either authoritarian or democratic political systems. Specifically, Lipset found a strong relationship between level of affluence and type of political system, demonstrating that less-affluent countries seldom establish democratic structures.

Behavioralism also influenced international relations, though it did not achieve the same dominance in this area that it enjoyed in domestic and comparative politics. The Correlates of War Project, founded at the University of Michigan in 1963, gathered much quantitative data and became one of the leading sources for scholars studying the causes and effects of war and international tension. Behavioralism also established itself in studies of judicial and bureaucratic systems.

By the 1960s behavioralism was in full bloom, forcing the traditionalists into retreat in much of the discipline. By the late 1960s, however, criticism of behavioralism had begun to grow. One charge leveled against it was that the statistical correlations uncovered by behavioral studies did not always establish which variable, if any, was the cause and which the effect. The fact that two variables change together does not in itself show which causes which; indeed, the changes exhibited by both variables may be the effects of an underlying third variable. In order to make sense of the actual relationship between the variables, the researcher must often use intuition—a tool that behavioralists expressly sought to avoid. A study of white blue-collar Roman Catholics in Detroit, Mich., for example, might find that during a certain period they were more likely to vote Republican as they became more affluent and suburbanized. However, whether the change in their voting patterns was due to their race, their religion, their increased affluence, or their suburban lifestyle—or whether they simply responded to the message or personality of particular Republican Party candidates—may be unclear.

In addition, though behavioral research yielded important insights into the political behaviour of individuals, it often explained little about actual governance. Voting studies, for example, rarely provided an understanding of public policy. Because behavioral research tended to be limited to topics that were amenable to quantitative study, it was often dismissed as narrow and irrelevant to major political issues. Indeed, intense methodological debates among behavioralists (and within the discipline more broadly) often seemed arcane, filled with esoteric jargon and addressed to issues of little concern to most citizens. Because behavioralists needed quantitative survey and electoral data, which were often unavailable in dictatorships or less-affluent countries, their approach was useless in many parts of the world. In addition, the reliability of behavioral research was called into question by its dependence in large part on verbal responses to questionnaires. Analyses of survey results have shown that respondents often give socially desirable answers and are likely to conceal their true feelings on controversial topics; moreover, the wording of questions, as well as the ordering of possible answers, can affect the results, making concrete conclusions difficult. Finally, many behavioral findings revealed nothing new but simply restated well-established or obvious conclusions, such as the observation that wealthy people tend to vote conservative and poor and working-class people tend to vote liberal or left-of-centre. For all of these reasons, behavioralism did not become the sole methodology in political science, and many behavioralists eventually acknowledged the need for the unquantified insights of traditionalists; by the late 1960s political scientists called this the "postbehavioral synthesis."

# BEHAVIOURISM

Behaviourism was a highly influential academic school of psychology that dominated psychological theory between the two world wars. Classical behaviourism, prevalent in the first third of the 20th century, was concerned exclusively with measurable and observable data and excluded ideas, emotions, and the consideration of inner mental experience and activity in general. In behaviourism, the organism is seen as "responding" to conditions (stimuli) set by the outer environment and by inner biological processes.

The previously dominant school of thought, structuralism, conceived of psychology as the science of consciousness, experience, or mind; although bodily activities were not excluded, they were considered significant chiefly in their relations to mental phenomena. The characteristic method of structuralism was thus introspection—observing and reporting on the working of one's own mind.

The early formulations of behaviourism were a reaction by U.S. psychologist John B. Watson against the introspective psychologies. In *Behaviorism* (1924), Watson wrote that "Behaviorism claims that 'consciousness' is neither a definable nor a usable concept; that it is merely another word for the 'soul' of more ancient times." Thus introspection was to be discarded; only such observations were to be considered admissible as could be made by independent observers of the same object or event—exactly as in physics or chemistry. In this way psychology was to become, in Watson's words, "a purely objective, experimental branch of natural science."

Watson's desire to "bury subjective subject matter" received widespread support. Between the early 1920s and mid-century, the methods of behaviourism dominated U.S. psychology and had wide international repercussions. Although the chief alternatives to behaviourism (e.g., Gestalt psychology, which emphasized individuals' perceptual and cognitive experience taken as a whole, and psychoanalysis, which focused on unconscious mental processes) advocated methods based on data derived from experience, even these alternatives accommodated Watson's approach by emphasizing a need for objective validation of experience-based hypotheses.

The period 1912–1930 (roughly) may be called that of classical behaviourism, which was dedicated to proving that phenomena formerly believed to require introspective study (such as thinking, imagery, emotions, or feeling) might be understood in terms of stimulus and response. Classical behaviourism was further characterized by a strict determinism based on the belief that every response is elicited by a specific stimulus.

*Behavioral psychologist B.F. Skinner at Harvard University, training a rat to press a lever and be rewarded with food.* Nina Leen/ Time & Life Pictures/Getty Images

A derivative form of classical behaviourism known as neobe-haviourism evolved from 1930 through the late 1940s. In this approach, psychologists attempted to translate the general methodology prescribed by Watson into a detailed, experimentally based theory of adaptive behaviour. This era was dominated by learning theorists Clark L. Hull and B.F. Skinner; Skinner's thought was the direct descendant of Watson's intellectual heritage and became dominant in the field after the mid-1950s.

The emphasis on the objective remained fundamentally the same, even while admitting the existence of intervening (i.e., mental) variables, accepting verbal reports, and branching into areas such as perception. A natural outgrowth of behaviourist theory was behaviour therapy, which rose to prominence after World War II and focused on modifying observable behaviour, rather than the thoughts and feelings of the patient (as in psychoanalysis).

## POLITICAL CULTURE

Political culture may be defined as the political psychology of a country or nation (or subgroup thereof). Political culture studies attempt to uncover deep-seated, long-held values characteristic of a society or group rather than ephemeral attitudes toward specific issues that might be gathered through public-opinion surveys. Several major studies using a political culture approach appeared simultaneously with the behavioral studies of the late 1950s, adding psychological and anthropological insights to statistical covariance. The study of political culture was hardly new; since at least the time of Plato, virtually all political thinkers have acknowledged the importance of what Alexis de Tocqueville called "habits of the heart" in making the political system work as it does.

Modern political culture approaches were motivated in part by a desire to understand the rise of totalitarian regimes in the 20th century in Russia, Germany, and Italy, and many early studies (e.g., *The Authoritarian Personality*) focused on Nazi Germany; one early political culture study, Edward Banfield's *The Moral Basis of a Backward Society* (1958), argued that poverty in southern Italy grew out of a psychological inability to trust or to form associations beyond the immediate family, a finding that was long controversial but is now accepted by many.

*Paul von Hindenburg (center, right), second president of the Weimar Republic. Political instability during Hindenburg's second term gave rise to the political culture that brought Adolf Hitler and the Nazi Party to power.* Central Press/Hulton Archive/ Getty Images

Perhaps the most important work of political culture was Gabriel Almond and Sidney Verba's *The Civic Culture: Political Attitudes and Democracy in Five Nations* (1963), which surveyed 1,000-person samples in the United States, the United Kingdom, West Germany, Italy, and Mexico. Almond and Verba identified three types of political culture: (1) participant, in which citizens understand and take part in politics and voluntary associations, (2) subject, in which citizens largely obey but participate little, and (3) parochial, in which citizens have neither knowledge of nor interest in politics. The authors found that democratic stability arises from a balance or mixture of these cultures, a conclusion similar to that drawn by Aristotle. In Almond and Verba's edited volume *The Civic Culture Revisited* (1980), several authors demonstrated that political culture in each of their subject countries was undergoing major change, little of which was predictable from the original study, suggesting that political culture, while more durable than mere public opinion, is never static. Critics of *The Civic Culture* also pointed out that political structures can affect culture. The effective governance and economic policies of West Germany's government made that country's citizens embrace democracy, whereas Britain's economic decline made Britons more cynical about politics. The problem, again, is determining causality.

Over the decades Lipset, who served as president of both the American Sociological Association and the American Political Science Association, turned from explanations of political values based on social class to those based on history and culture, which, he argued, displayed consistency throughout history. American political scientist Robert Putnam followed in this Tocquevillian tradition in *Making Democracy Work: Civic Traditions in*

*Modern Italy* (1993), which demonstrated that the historical cultures of Italy's regions explain their current political situations. In *Bowling Alone: The Collapse and Revival of American Community* (2000), Putnam claimed that the American tendency to form citizen groups, a characteristic that Tocqueville praised, was weakening. Americans were less often joining groups and participating in politics, Putnam argued, leading to a loss of "social capital" (the collective value of social networks) and potentially undermining democracy, a worry shared by other political observers in the United States.

Adopting what became known as the "path-dependent development" approach, advocates of the historical-cultural school maintained that contemporary society is a reflection of society in ages past. The political culture approach declined in the 1970s but was later revived as political scientists incorporated it into explanations of why some countries experienced economic growth and established democratic political systems while others did not. Some suggested that the rapid economic growth and democratization that took place in some East Asian countries in the second half of the 20th century was facilitated by a political culture based on Confucianism. In Africa and Latin America, they argued, the absence of a culture that valued hard work and capital accumulation led to the stagnation of much of those regions. This viewpoint was captured by the title of Lawrence E. Harrison and Samuel P. Huntington's edited volume *Culture Matters: How Values Shape Human Progress* (2000).

## SYSTEMS ANALYSIS

Systems analysis, which was influenced by the Austrian-Canadian biologist Ludwig von Bertalanffy and the

American sociologist Talcott Parsons (1902–1979), is a broad descriptive theory of how the various parts and levels of a political system interact with each other. The central idea of systems analysis is based on an analogy with biology: just as the heart, lungs, and blood function as a whole, so do the components of social and political systems. When one component changes or comes under stress, the other components will adjust to compensate.

Systems analysis studies first appeared alongside behavioral and political culture studies in the 1950s. A groundbreaking work employing the approach, David Easton's *The Political System* (1953), conceived the political system as integrating all activities through which social policy is formulated and executed—that is, the political system is the policy-making process. Easton defined political behaviour as the "authoritative allocation of values," or the distribution of rewards in wealth, power, and status that the system may provide. In doing so, he distinguished his sense of the subject matter of political science from that of Lasswell, who had argued that political science is concerned with the distribution and content of patterns of value throughout society. Easton's conception of system emphasizes linkages between the system and its environment. Inputs (demands) flow into the system and are converted into outputs (decisions and actions) that constitute the authoritative allocation of values. Drawing on cybernetics (the application of mathematics to the control of complex physical processes and systems), the Czech-born American political scientist Karl Deutsch used a systems perspective to view the political system as a communications network. Following Deutsch, some political scientists tried briefly to establish communications as the basis of politics.

Systems analysis was applied to international relations to explain how the forces of the international system affect the behaviour of states. The American political scientist Morton Kaplan delineated types of international systems and their logical consequences in *System and Process in International Politics* (1957). According to Kaplan, for example, the Cold War rivalry between the United States and the Soviet Union brought about a bipolar international system that governed much of the two countries' foreign and security policies. Locked in a zero-sum game (when one country wins, the other loses), the two superpowers watched each other vigilantly, eager for gains but also wary of the threat of nuclear war.

In *Man, the State, and War* (1959), the American international relations theorist Kenneth Waltz applied systems theory to the study of international conflict to develop a view known as structural realism. Waltz argued that the underlying cause of war is an anarchic international system in which there is no recognized authority for resolving conflicts between sovereign states. According to Waltz:

> *with many sovereign states, with no system of law enforceable among them, with each state judging its grievances and ambitions according to the dictates of its own reason or desire—conflict, sometimes leading to war, is bound to occur.*

By the 1970s, systems approaches to domestic politics were criticized and generally abandoned as unverifiable abstractions of little explanatory or predictive power. (In international politics, however, systems approaches remained important.) On closer examination, the "conversion process" of systems theory—i.e., the transformation of inputs into outputs—struck many as simply plain old "politics." Another problem was that much of systems theory took as its norm and model an idealized version of American politics that did not apply universally to the domestic politics of all societies. Systems analysis also was unable to explain certain policy decisions that were made despite the absence of predominating favourable inputs, such as the decision by U.S. Pres. Lyndon B. Johnson to deepen U.S. involvement in the war in Vietnam. Finally, systems theorists unrealistically reified the systems of the countries they studied, portraying them as durable and stable because they were supposed to correct and reform themselves. They were thus unable to explain defective systems or systemic upheavals, such as the collapse of communist regimes in eastern and central Europe in 1989–91.

Other approaches employing systems analysis flourished briefly in the late 20th century. Decision-making theory is based on systems theory but also borrows from game theory, which was devised by mathematicians during World War II. Decision-making theory supposes that actors behave rationally to achieve goals by selecting the course of action that will maximize benefits and minimize costs. This assumption has been contradicted by some studies, such as Graham Allison's *Essence of Decision* (1971), which found that the decision-making process of the administration of U.S. Pres. John F. Kennedy during the Cuban missile crisis could not be adequately explained in terms of a strict rational calculation of costs and benefits; instead, decisions often depended on the standard operating procedures of organizational actors and the information that subordinates fed to their superiors, which itself was skewed by "bureaucratic politics." Allison argued that one key determinant of Kennedy's decision to impose a naval blockade on Cuba rather than to invade the island was the delayed flight of a spy plane, which resulted from a quarrel between the Central Intelligence Agency and the U.S. Air Force over who was to pilot the plane. (Allison's view was refuted by subsequent studies that showed that Kennedy had decided in advance not to bomb or invade Cuba.) Bureaucratic-process models, which maintain that policy decisions are influenced by the priorities of bureaucrats who compete with each other to protect their programs, budgets, and procedures, became prominent during the 1970s, but research failed to identify a consistent pattern of influence resulting from bureaucratic infighting.

There was no consensus among political scientists concerning the system that developed after the end of the Cold War. Some scholars believed that there was a return to a 19th-century balance-of-power system, in which multiple states make and remake alliances. Others argued for the existence of a multipolar system consisting of trade blocs that were neither mutually hostile nor totally cooperative with each other. Some argued that the international system became unipolar, the United States being the single dominant world power. Huntington, in a controversial article published in 1993 and a book, *The Clash of Civilizations and the Remaking of World Order*, published in 1996, used cultural theory to propose that the emerging international system constituted a "clash of civilizations." Several civilizations, each based mostly on religion, variously clashed and cooperated. The worst clashes, he argued, took place between Islamic and other civilizations. Many scholars rejected Huntington's analysis as simplistic and ill-informed, but others found it persuasive, especially after the September 11 attacks in the United States in 2001 and the subsequent U.S.-British invasion of Afghanistan (2001) and the U.S.-led attack on Iraq (2003), both of which led to prolonged conflicts in those countries.

# THE THEORY OF RATIONAL CHOICE

The dominant school of thought in political science in the late 20th century was rational choice theory. For rational choice theorists, history and culture are irrelevant to understanding political behaviour; instead, it is sufficient to know the actors' interests and to assume that they pursue them rationally. Whereas the earlier decision-making approach sought to explain the decisions of elite groups (mostly in matters of foreign policy), rational choice theorists attempted to apply their far more formal theory (which sometimes involved the use of mathematical notation) to all facets of political life. Many believed they had found the key that would at last make political science truly scientific. In *An Economic Theory of Democracy* (1957), an early work in rational choice theory, Anthony Downs claimed that significant elements of political life could be explained in terms of voter self-interest. Downs showed that in democracies the aggregate distribution of political opinion forms a bell-shaped curve, with most voters possessing moderate opinions; he argued that this fact forces political parties in democracies to adopt centrist positions. The founder of rational choice theory was William Riker, who applied economic and game-theoretic approaches to develop increasingly complex mathematical models of politics. In *The Theory of Political Coalitions* (1962), Riker demonstrated by mathematical reasoning why and how politicians form alliances. Riker and his followers applied this version of rational choice theory—which they variously called rational choice, public choice, social choice, formal modeling, or positive political theory—to explain almost everything, including voting, legislation, wars, and bureaucracy. Some researchers used games to reproduce key decisions in small-group experiments.

Rational choice theory identified—or rediscovered—at least two major explanatory factors that some political scientists had neglected: (1) that politicians are endlessly opportunistic and (2) that all decisions take place in some type of institutional setting. Rational choice theorists argued that political institutions structure the opportunities available to politicians and thus help to explain their actions.

By the early 21st century, rational choice theory was being stiffly challenged. Critics alleged that it simply mathematized the obvious and, in searching for universal patterns, ignored important cultural contexts, which thus rendered it unable to predict much of importance; another charge was that the choices the theory sought to explain appeared "rational" only in retrospect. Reacting to such criticisms, some rational choice theorists began calling themselves "new institutionalists" or "structuralists" to emphasize their view that all political choices take place within specific institutional structures. U.S. Congress members, for example, typically calculate how their votes on bills will help or hurt their chances for reelection. In this way, rational choice theory led political science back to its traditional concern with political institutions, such as parliaments and laws. In more recent years, increasing numbers of rational choice theorists have backed away from claims that their approach is capable of explaining every political phenomenon.

## DEMOCRATIC THEORY

Late in the 20th century, some political scientists rediscovered their Aristotelian roots by returning to the question of how to achieve the good, just, and stable polity—that is, by returning to the study of democracy. Although the approaches taken were highly diverse, most researchers attempted to identify the factors by which democracies are established and sustained. Democratic theory was revived in earnest in the late 1980s, when communist regimes were collapsing throughout eastern Europe, and was accompanied by the founding of the influential *Journal of Democracy* in 1990.

The American political theorist Robert Dahl, who had long been a scholar of the topic, viewed democracy as the pluralist interplay of groups in what he called a "polyarchy." Historical-cultural thinkers such as Lipset traced the origins of democracy to the values that democratic societies developed long ago. Samuel Huntington, perhaps the most influential post-World War II American political scientist, worried about a "democratic distemper" in which citizens demand more than the system can deliver. Huntington also viewed democracy as coming in waves—the most recent having started in 1974 in Greece and Portugal and having subsequently washed over Spain and Latin America—but warned of a potential reverse wave toward authoritarianism. The Spanish American political scientist Juan Linz explored how democracies can decline, and the Dutch-born American scholar Arend Lijphart considered the institutional arrangements (political parties and electoral systems, executives and parliaments) that were most likely to produce stable political systems.

Modernization theorists noted the connection between democracy and economic development but were unable to determine whether economic development typically precedes democracy or vice versa. Few of them regarded democracy as inevitable, and many noted its philosophical, psychological, and social prerequisites, suggesting that democracy may be a largely Western phenomenon that is not easily transplanted to non-Western cultures. Others, however, argued that democracy is a universal value that transcends culture. Some worried that the legitimacy of established democracies was eroding in the late 20th and early 21st centuries, as citizens became disenchanted with the political process and many moved away from political participation in favour of private pursuits. Voter turnout fell in most countries, in part because citizens saw little difference between the major political parties, believing them to be essentially power-seeking and self-serving. Some attributed this trend to a supposed abandonment of ideology as most parties hewed to centrist positions in order to capture the large moderate vote. Still others argued that party systems, ossified for at least a generation and based on social and political conflicts that had long been resolved, failed to address in a coherent fashion new social issues (e.g., feminism, environmentalism, civil rights) that concerned many citizens. Some blamed the media for focusing on political scandals instead of issues of substance, and some cited the inability of governments to fully address society's ills (e.g., crime, drug abuse, unemployment).

Nevertheless, not all scholars viewed this change with alarm. Some argued that citizens were generally better-educated and more critical than they were given credit for, that they were simply demanding better, cleaner government, and that these demands would eventually lead to long-term democratic renewal.

## ENDURING DEBATES

Political scientists, like other social and natural scientists, gather data and formulate theories. The two tasks are often out of balance, however, leading either to the collection of irrelevant facts or to the construction of misleading theories. Throughout the post-World War II era, political scientists developed and discarded numerous theories, and there was considerable (and unresolved) debate as to whether it is more important to develop theories and then collect data to confirm or reject them or to collect and analyze data from which theories would flow.

Perhaps the oldest philosophical dispute has to do with the relative importance of subjectivity and objectivity. Many political scientists have attempted to develop approaches that are value-free and wholly objective. In modern political science, much of this debate takes place between structuralists and cultural theorists. Structuralists claim that the way in which the world is organized (or structured) determines politics and that the proper objects of study for political science are power, interests, and institutions, which they construe as objective features of political life. In contrast, cultural theorists, who study values, opinions, and psychology, argue that subjective perceptions of reality are more important than objective reality itself. However, most scholars now believe that the two realms feed into one another and cannot be totally separated. To explain the apparent inertia of Japan's political system, for example, a structuralist would cite the country's electoral laws and powerful ministries, whereas a cultural theorist would look to deeply rooted Japanese values such as obedience and stability. Few in one camp, however, would totally dismiss the arguments of the other.

Likewise, although some political scientists continue to insist that only quantified data are legitimate, some topics are not amenable to study in these terms. The decisions of top officials, for example, are often made in small groups and behind closed doors, and so understanding them requires subjective descriptive material based on interviews and observations—essentially the techniques of good journalists. If done well, these subjective studies may be more valid and longer-lived than quantitative studies.

*Japanese Emperor Akihito (left) meets with kimono-clad astronaut Naoko Yamazaki (third from the right) at Akasaka Imperial Garden in Tokyo in October 2010. Many find Japan's political culture conservative and traditional.* Kazuhiro Nogi/AFP/Getty Images

Prior to the development of reliable survey research, most political analyses focused on elites. Once a sizable amount of research had become available, there was a considerable debate about whether rulers are guided by citizen preferences, expressed through interest groups and elections, or whether elites pursue their own goals and manipulate public opinion to achieve their ends.

Despite numerous studies of public opinion, voting behaviour, and interest groups, the issue has not been resolved and, indeed, is perhaps unresolvable. Analyses can establish statistical relationships, but it has been difficult to demonstrate causality with any certainty. This debate is complicated by two factors. First, although there is a considerable body of survey and electoral data, most people ignore politics most of the time, a factor that must be considered in attempting to understand which part of the "public" policy makers listen to—all citizens, all voters, or only those expressing an intense view on a particular matter. Political analyses based on elites are hindered by a dearth of reliable elite-level data, as researchers are rarely invited into the deliberations of rulers. Accordingly, much is known about the social bases of politics but little of how and why decisions are made. Even when decision makers grant interviews or write their memoirs, firm conclusions remain elusive, because officials often provide accounts that are self-serving or misleading.

Political science has had difficulty handling rapid change; it prefers the static (stable political systems) to the dynamic. If historians are stuck in the past, political scientists are often captives of the present. For some the collapse of the Soviet Union showed that the theories and methods of political science are of only limited utility. Despite decades of gathering data and theorizing, political science was unable to anticipate the defining event of the post-World War II era. Critics charged that political science could describe what is but could never discern what was likely to be. Others, however, maintained that this criticism was unfair, arguing that such upheavals can be predicted, given sufficient data. Still, the demise of the Soviet Union spurred some political scientists to develop theories to explain political

*West Berliners watching as a section of the Berlin Wall is demolished in 1989. Political upheaval such as the fall of communism in Europe is a subject of debate in the political science arena.* AFP/ Getty Images

changes and transformations. Examining the collapse of authoritarian regimes and their replacement with democratic governments in Greece, Spain, Portugal, Latin America, eastern Europe, and the Soviet Union during the last three decades of the 20th century, they sought to develop a theory of transitions to democracy. Others argued that no such universal theory is possible and that all democratic transitions are unique.

At the beginning of the 21st century, political science was faced with a stark dilemma: the more scientific it tried to be, the more removed it found itself from the burning issues of the day. Although some research in political science would continue to be arcane and unintelligible to the layperson and even to other scholars, many political scientists attempted to steer a middle course, one that maintained a rigorous scientific approach but also addressed questions that are important to academics, citizens, and decision makers alike. Indeed, some political scientists, recognizing that many "scientific" approaches had lost their utility after a decade or two, suggested that the discipline should cease its attempts to imitate the natural sciences and return to the classic concerns of analyzing and promoting the political good.

# CHAPTER 4

## Political Philosophy: From Antiquity to the End of the Middle Ages

A lthough in antiquity great civilizations arose in Egypt and Mesopotamia, in the Indus Valley, and in China, there was little speculation about the problems of political philosophy as formulated in the West. The Code of Hammurabi (*c.* 1750 BCE) consists of rules propounded by the Babylonian ruler Hammurabi as a representative of God on Earth and is mainly concerned with order, trade, and property; the *Maxims of Ptahhotep* (*c.* 2300 BCE) contains shrewd advice from the Egyptian vizier on how to prosper in a bureaucracy; and the *Artha-sastra* of Kautilya, grand vizier to Chandragupta Maurya in the late 4th century BCE, is a set of Machiavellian precepts on how to survive under an arbitrary power. To be sure, the Buddhist concept of dharma (social custom and duty), which inspired the Indian emperor Asoka in the 3rd century BCE, implies a moralization of public power, and the teachings of Confucius in the 6th century BCE are a code of conduct designed to stabilize society, but there is not, outside Europe, much speculation about the basis of political obligation and the purpose of the state, with both of which Western political philosophy is mainly concerned. An authoritarian society is taken for granted, backed by religious sanctions, and a conservative and arbitrary power is generally accepted.

In contrast to this overwhelming conservatism, paralleled by the rule of custom and tribal elders in most primitive societies, the political philosophers of ancient Greece question the basis and purpose of government. Though they do not separate political speculation from shrewd observations that today would be regarded as political science, they created the vocabulary of Western political thought.

## PLATO

The first elaborate work of European political philosophy is the *Republic* of Plato, a masterpiece of insight and feeling, superbly expressed in dialogue form and probably meant for recitation. Further development of Plato's ideas is undertaken in his *Statesman* and *Laws*, the latter prescribing the ruthless methods whereby they might be imposed. Plato grew up during the great Peloponnesian War between Athens and Sparta and, like many political philosophers, tried to find remedies for prevalent political injustice and decline. Indeed, the *Republic* is the first of the utopias, though not one of the more attractive, and it is the first classic attempt of a European philosopher to moralize political life.

Books V, VII–VIII, and IX of the *Republic* are cast as a lively discussion between Socrates, whose wisdom Plato is recounting, and various leisured Athenians. They state the major themes of political philosophy with poetic power. Plato's work has been criticized as static and class-bound, reflecting the moral and aesthetic assumptions of an elite in a slave-owning civilization and bound by the narrow limits of the city-state (polis). The work is indeed a classic example of a philosopher's vivisection of society, imposing by relatively humane means the rule of a high-minded minority.

The *Republic* is a criticism of current Hellenic politics—often an indictment. It is based upon a metaphysical act of faith, for Plato believes that a world of permanent Forms exists beyond the limitations of human experience and that morality and the good life, which the state should promote, are reflections of these ideal entities. The point is best made in the famous simile of the cave, in which humans are chained with their faces to the wall and their backs to the light, so that they see only the shadows of reality. So constrained, they shrink from what is truly "real" and permanent and need to be forced to face it. This idealistic doctrine, known misleadingly as realism, pervades all of Plato's philosophy: its opposite doctrine, nominalism, declares that only particular and observed "named" data are accessible to the mind. On his realist assumption, Plato regards most ordinary life as illusion and the current evils of politics as the result of the human pursuit of brute instinct. It follows that:

> *unless philosophers bear kingly rule in cities or those who are now called kings and princes become genuine and adequate philosophers, and political power and philosophy are brought together...there will be no respite from evil for cities.*

Only philosopher-statesmen can apprehend permanent and transcendent Forms and turn to "face the brightest blaze of being" outside the cave, and only philosophically minded people of action can be the saviours and helpers of the citizens.

Plato is thus indirectly the pioneer of modern beliefs that only a party organization, inspired by correct and "scientific" doctrines, formulated by the written word and interpreted by authority, can rightly guide the state. His rulers would form an elite, not responsible to the mass of the people. Thus, in spite of his high moral purpose, he has been called an enemy of the open society and the father of totalitarianism. But he is also an anatomist of the evils of unbridled appetite and political corruption and insists on the need to use public power to moral ends.

Having described his utopia, Plato turns to analyze the existing types of government in human terms with great insight. Monarchy is the best but impracticable; in oligarchies the rule of the few and the pursuit of wealth divide societies—the rich become demoralized and the poor envious, and there is no harmony in the state. In democracy, in which the poor get the upper hand, demagogues distribute "a peculiar kind of equality to equals and unequals impartially," and the old flatter the young, fawning on their juniors to avoid the appearance of being sour or despotic. The leaders plunder the propertied classes and divide the spoils between themselves and the people until confusion and corruption lead to tyranny, an even worse form of government, for the tyrant becomes a wolf instead of a man and "lops off" potential rivals and starts wars to distract the people from their discontent. "Then, by Zeus," Plato concludes, "the public learns what a monster they have begotten."

In the *Statesman* Plato admits that, although there is a correct science of government, like geometry it cannot be realized, and he stresses the need for the rule of law, since no ruler can be trusted with unbridled power. He then examines which of the current forms of government is the least difficult to live with, for the ruler, after all, is an artist who has to work within the limits of his medium. In the *Laws*, purporting to be a discussion of how best to found a polis in Crete, he presents a detailed program in which a state with some 5,000 citizens is ruled by 37 curators of laws and a council of 360. But the keystone of the arch is a sinister and secret Nocturnal Council to be "the sheet anchor of the state," established in its "central fortress as guardian." Poets and musicians will be discouraged and the young subjected to a rigid, austere, and exacting education.

The stark consequence of Plato's political philosophy here becomes apparent. He had, nonetheless, stated, in the dawn of European political thought, the normative principle that the state should aim at promoting the good life and social harmony and that the rule of law, in the absence of the rule of philosopher-kings, is essential to this purpose.

# ARISTOTLE

Aristotle, who was a pupil in the Academy of Plato, remarks that "all the writings of Plato are original: they show ingenuity, novelty of view and a spirit of enquiry. But perfection in everything is perhaps a difficult thing." Aristotle was a scientist rather than a prophet, and his *Politics*, written while he was teaching at the Lyceum at Athens, is only part of an encyclopaedic account of nature and society, in which he analyzes society as if he were a doctor and prescribes remedies for its ills. Political behaviour is here regarded as a branch of biology as well as of ethics; in contrast to Plato, Aristotle was an empirical political philosopher. He criticizes many of Plato's ideas as impracticable, but, like Plato, he admires balance and moderation and aims at a harmonious city under the rule of law. The book is composed of lecture notes and is arranged in a confusing way—a quarry of arguments and definitions of great value but hard to master. The first book, though probably the last written, is a general introduction; Books II, III, and VII–VIII, probably the earliest, deal with the ideal state; and Books IV–VII analyze actual states and politics. The treatise is thus, in modern terms, a mixture of political philosophy and political science.

Like Plato, Aristotle thinks in terms of the city-state, which he regards as the natural form of civilized life, social and political, and the best medium in which human capacities can be realized. Hence his famous definition of man as a "political animal," distinguished from the other animals by his gift of speech and power of moral judgment. "Man, when perfected," he writes:

> *is the best of animals, but when separated from law and justice he is the worst of all, since armed injustice is the most dangerous, and he is equipped at birth with the arms of intelligence and wit, moral qualities which he may use for the worst ends.*

Since all nature is pervaded by purpose and since humans "aim at the good," the city-state, which is the highest form of human community, aims at the highest good. Like sailors with their separate functions, who yet have a common object in safety in navigation, citizens, too, have a common aim—in modern terms survival, security, and the enhancement of the quality of life. In the context of the city-state, this high quality of life can be realized only by a minority, and Aristotle, like Plato, excludes those who are not full citizens or who are slaves; indeed, he says that some men are "slaves by nature" and deserve their status. Plato and Aristotle aim at an aristocratic and exacting way of life, reflecting, in more sophisticated forms, the ideas of the warrior aristocracies depicted by the epic poet Homer.

Having stated that the aim of the city-state is to promote the good life, Aristotle insists that it can be achieved only under the rule of law.

> *The rule of law is preferable to that of a single citizen; if it be the better course to have individuals ruling, they should be made law guardians or ministers of the laws.*

The rule of law is better than that even of the best men, for:

> *he who bids law rule may be deemed to bid God and reason alone rule, but he who bids men rule adds the element of the beast; for desire is a wild beast, and passion perverts the minds of rulers, even if they are the best of men.*

This doctrine, which distinguishes between lawful government and tyranny, survived the Middle Ages and, by subjecting the ruler to law, became the theoretical sanction of modern constitutional government.

Aristotle also vindicates the rule of custom and justifies the obligations accepted by members of society: the solitary man, he writes, "is either a beast or a God." This outlook at once reflects the respect for custom and solidarity that has promoted survival in primitive tribal societies, even at the price of sacrificing individuals, and gives a theoretical justification for the acceptance of political obligation.

Like Plato, Aristotle analyzes the different kinds of city-states. While states are bound, like animals, to be different, he considers a balanced "mixed" constitution the best—it reflects the ideal of justice (*dikē*) and fair dealing, which gives every individual his due in a conservative social order in which citizens of the middle condition preponderate. And he attacks oligarchy, democracy, and tyranny. Under democracy, he argues, demagogues attain power by bribing the electorate and waste accumulated wealth. But it is tyranny that Aristotle most detests; the arbitrary power of an individual above the law who is:

> *responsible to no-one and who governs all alike with a view to his own advantage and not of his subjects, and therefore against their will. No free man can endure such a government.*

The *Politics* contains not only a firm statement of these principles but also a penetrating analysis of how city-states are governed, as well as of the causes of revolutions, in which "inferiors revolt in order that they may be equal, and equals that they may be superior." The treatise concludes with an elaborate plan for educating the citizens to attain the "mean," the "possible," and the "becoming." The first implies a balanced development of body and mind, ability and imagination; the second, the recognition of the limits of mind and the range and limitations of talent; the third, an outcome of the other two, is the style and self-assurance that come from the resulting self-control and confidence.

While, therefore, Aristotle accepts a conservative and hierarchical social order, he states firmly that public power should aim at promoting the good life and that only through the rule of law and justice can the good life be attained. These principles were novel in the context of his time, when the great extra-European civilizations were ruled, justly or unjustly, by the arbitrary power of semi-divine rulers and when other peoples, though respecting tribal custom and the authority of tribal elders, were increasingly organized under war leaders for depredation of other lands.

## CICERO AND THE STOICS

Both Plato and Aristotle had thought in terms of the city-state. But Aristotle's pupil Alexander the Great swamped the cities of old Greece and brought them into a vast empire that included Egypt, Persia, and the eastern coast of the Mediterranean. Although city-states remained the locus of the civilization of antiquity, they became part of an imperial power that broke up into kingdoms under Alexander's successors. This imperial power was reasserted on an even greater scale by Rome, whose empire at its greatest extent reached from central Scotland to the Euphrates River in what is now Iraq, and from Spain to eastern Anatolia (the Turkish peninsula). Civilization itself became identified with empire, and the development of eastern and western Europe was conditioned by it.

Since the city-state was no longer self-sufficient, universal philosophies developed that gave people something to live by in a wider world. Of these philosophies, Stoicism and Epicureanism were the most influential. The former inspired a rather grim self-sufficiency and sense of duty, as exemplified by the writings of the Roman emperor Marcus Aurelius; the latter, a prudent withdrawal from the world of affairs.

The setting for political philosophy thus became much wider, relating individuals to universal empire—thought of, as in China, as coterminous with civilization itself. Its inspiration remained Hellenic, but derivative Roman philosophers reinterpreted it, and Roman legal scholars enclosed the old concepts of political justice in a carapace of legal definitions, capable of surviving their civilization's decline.

The Roman orator Cicero lived during the 1st century BCE, a time of political confusion in which the old institutions of the republic were breaking down before military dictators. His *De republica* and *De legibus* (*Laws*) are both dialogues and reflect the Classical sense of purpose: "to make human life better by our thought and effort." Cicero defined the republic as an association held together by law; he further asserted, as Plato had maintained with his doctrine of Forms, that government was sanctioned by a universal natural law that reflected the cosmic order. Cicero expresses the pre-Christian Stoic attempt to moralize public power, apparent in the exacting sense of public responsibility shown by the emperors Hadrian and Marcus Aurelius in the 2nd century CE.

# MARCUS AURELIUS

(b. April 26, 121 CE, Rome—d. March 17, 180,
Vindobona [Vienna] or Sirmium, Pannonia)

Marcus Aurelius was emperor of Rome from 161 to 180. He was born into a wealthy and prominent family. The emperor Hadrian arranged that Marcus and Lucius Verus be adopted by the designated future emperor Antoninus Pius, who dutifully groomed Marcus as his heir. On his accession, Marcus nevertheless shared power with his adoptive brother as coemperor, though he himself remained the more dominant. His reign was marked by numerous military crises, all the major frontiers being threatened by invasion. Struggles against the Parthians (162–166) were successful, but returning troops brought a devastating plague to Rome. With a concurrent German invasion, Roman morale declined; the Germans were repulsed, but Verus died during the campaign (169). Though a man of gentle character and wide learning, Marcus opposed Christianity and supported persecution of its adherents. His *Meditations*, considered one of the great books of all times, gives a full picture of his philosophical beliefs and moral values.

To what extent he intended the *Meditations* for eyes other than his own is uncertain; they are fragmentary notes, discursive and epigrammatic by turn, of his reflections in the midst of campaigning and administration. In a way, it seems, he wrote them to nerve himself for his daunting responsibilities. Strikingly, though they comprise the innermost thoughts of a Roman, the *Meditations* were written in Greek—to such an extent had the union of cultures become a reality. Marcus was forever proposing to himself unattainable goals of conduct, forever contemplating the triviality, brutishness, and transience of the physical world and of humanity in general and himself in particular; otherworldly,

*Statue of Marcus Aurelius in Rome. Marcus Aurelius exem-plified the philosophy known as Stoicism, which emphasized self-sufficiency and duty.* Patrick Hertzog/AFP/Getty Images

yet believing in no other world, he was therefore tied to duty and service with no hope, even of everlasting fame, to sustain him. More certain and more important is the point that Marcus's anxieties reflect, in an exaggerated manner, the ethos of his age.

The *Meditations,* the thoughts of a philosopher-king, are basically the moral tenets of Stoicism, learned from Epictetus: the cosmos is a unity governed by an intelligence, and the human soul is a part of that divine intelligence and can therefore stand, if naked and alone, at least pure and undefiled, amid chaos and futility. Marcus Aurelius's reign is often thought to mark the Golden Age of Rome.

# AUGUSTINE OF HIPPO

When Christianity became the predominant creed of the empire under Constantine (converted 312) and the sole official religion under Theodosius (379–395), political philosophy changed profoundly. St. Augustine of Hippo's *City of God* (413–426/427), written when the empire was under attack by Germanic tribes, sums up and defines a new division between church and state and a conflict between "matter" and "spirit" resulting from original sin and the Fall of Man from the Garden of Eden.

St. Augustine, whose *Confessiones* (397) is a record of a new sort of introspection, combined a Classical and Judeo-Christian dualism. From the Stoics and the Roman epic poet Virgil he inherited an austere sense of duty, from Plato and the Neoplatonists a contempt for the illusions of appetite, and from the Pauline and patristic interpretation of Christianity a sense of the conflict between Light and Darkness that reflects Zoroastrian and Manichaean doctrines emanating from Persia. In this context worldly interests and government itself are dwarfed by the importance of attaining salvation and of escaping from an astrologically determined fate and from the demons who embody the darkness. Life becomes illuminated for the elect minority by the prospect of eternal salvation or, for those without grace, shrivels under the glare of eternal fires.

St. Augustine regarded salvation as predestinate and the cosmic process as designed to "gather" an elect to fill the places of the fallen angels and so "preserve and perhaps augment the number of the heavenly inhabitants." The role of government and indeed of society itself becomes subordinated to a "secular arm," part of an earthly city, as opposed to the "City of God." The function of government is to keep order in a world intrinsically evil.

Since Christianity had long played the main role in defense of the veneer of a precarious urban civilization in antiquity, this claim is not surprising. Constantine was a soldier putting to rights a breakdown in government, which nevertheless would continue in the West until the abdication of the last Western emperor in 476, though the Eastern half of the empire, subsequently known as the Byzantine Empire, would carry on with great wealth and power, centred on the new capital of Constantinople.

St. Augustine thus no longer assumed, as did Plato and Aristotle, that a harmonious and self-sufficient good life could be achieved within a properly organized city-state; he projected his political philosophy into a cosmic and lurid drama working out to a predestinate end. The normal interests and amenities of life became insignificant or disgusting, and the Christian church alone exercised a spiritual authority that could sanction government. This outlook, reinforced by the writings of other Church Fathers (the bishops and teachers of the early church), would long dominate medieval thought, for with the decline of civilization in the West the church became more completely the repository of learning and of the remnants of the old civilized life.

## THE EARLY MEDIEVAL PERIOD

The decline of ancient civilization in the West was severe. Although technology continued to develop (the horse collar, the stirrup, and the heavy plow came into use), intellectual pursuits, including political philosophy, became elementary.

In the Byzantine Empire, on the other hand, committees of jurists working for the emperor Justinian (reigned 527–565) produced the *Codex constitutionum* (*Constitutional Code*); the *Digesta* (*Digest*), or *Pandectae* (*Pandects*); the *Institutiones* (*Institutes*), which defined and condensed Roman law; and the *Novellae consitutiones post codicem* (new constitutions, referred to in English as the *Novels*); the four books are collectively known as the *Codex Justinianeus*, or *Code of Justinian*. The Byzantine basileus, or autocrat, had moral responsibility for guarding and harmonizing an elaborate state, a "colony" of heaven in which reason and not mere will ought to rule. This autocracy and the orthodox form of Christianity were inherited by the Christianized rulers of the Balkans, of Kievan Russia, and of Muscovy.

In the West, two essential principles of Hellenic and Christian political philosophy were transmitted, if only in elementary definitions, in rudimentary encyclopaedias. St. Isidore of Sevilla, in his 7th-century *Etymologiae* ("Etymologies"), for example, asserts that kings rule only on condition of doing right and that their rule reflects a Ciceronic law of nature "common to all people and mankind everywhere by natural instinct." Further, the Germanic tribes respected the civilization they took over and exploited; when converted, they revered the papacy. In 800 the Frankish ruler Charlemagne established a western European empire

The Emperor Charlemagne, whose Holy Roman Empire upheld the idea of a Christian empire in the West during the early medieval period. Archive Photos/Getty Images

482-565 𝔄.𝔇.

*Emperor Justinian and his wife, Queen Theodora. Justinian sponsored a codification of laws for the Byzantine Empire.* Buyenlarge/Archive Photos/Getty Images

that would eventually be called the Holy Roman Empire. The idea of a Christian empire coterminous with civilization thus survived in Western as well as Eastern Christendom.

## JOHN OF SALISBURY

After Augustine, no full-length speculative work of political philosophy appeared in the West until the *Policraticus* (1159), by John of Salisbury (1115/20-1180), a great Latin scholar who became bishop of Chartres, France. Based on John's wide Classical reading, it centres on the ideal ruler, who represents a "public power." John admired the Roman emperors Augustus and Trajan, and, in a still predominantly feudal world, his book carried on the Roman tradition of centralized authority, though without its Byzantine autocracy (a government in which one person possesses unlimited power). The prince, he insists, is he who rules in accordance with law, while a tyrant is one who oppresses the people by irresponsible power. This distinction, which derives from the Greeks, Cicero, and St. Augustine, is fundamental to Western concepts of liberty and the trusteeship of power.

John did not know Aristotle's *Politics*, but his learning is nevertheless remarkable, even if his political similes are unsophisticated. His favourite metaphor for the body politic is the human body: the place of the head is filled by the prince, who is subject only to God; the place of the heart is filled by the senate; the eyes, ears, and tongue are the judges, provincial governors, and soldiers; and the officials are the hands. The tax gatherers are the intestines and ought not to retain their accumulations too long, and the farmers and peasants are the feet. John also compares a commonwealth to a hive and even to a centipede. This vision of a centralized government, more appropriate to the memory of the Roman Empire than to a medieval monarchy, is a landmark of the 12th-century revival of speculative thought.

# THOMAS AQUINAS

It is a far cry from this practical 12th-century treatise by a man of affairs to the elaborate justification of Christian kingship and natural law created by St. Thomas Aquinas in the 13th century, during the climax of medieval Western civilization. His political philosophy is only part of a metaphysical construction of Aristotelian range—for Aristotle had now been assimilated from Arabic sources and given a new Christian content, with the added universality of the Stoic and Augustinian world outlook. Aquinas's *Summa theologiae* (1265/66–1273) purports to answer all the major questions of existence, including those of political philosophy. Like Aristotle, Aquinas thinks in terms of an ethical purpose. Natural law is discussed in the first part of the second book as part of the discussion of original sin and what would now be termed psychology, while war comes under the second part of the second book as an aspect of virtue and vice. Law is defined as "that which is regulation and measure." It is designed to promote the "felicity and beatitude" that are the ends of human life. Aquinas agrees with Aristotle that "the city is the perfection of community" and that the purpose of public power should be to promote the common good. The only legitimate power is from the community, which is the sole medium of human well-being. In his *De regimine principum* (1266; *On the Government of Princes*), he compares society to a ship in need of a helmsman and repeats Aristotle's definition of man as a social and political animal. Again following Aristotle, he considers oligarchy unjust and democracy evil. Rulers should aim to make the "life of the multitude good in accordance with the purpose of life which is heavenly happiness." They should also create peace, conserve life, and preserve the state—a threefold responsibility.

Here is a complete program for a hierarchical society within a cosmic order. It combines the Hellenic sense of purpose with Christian aims and asserts that, under God, power resides in the community, embodied in the ruler but only for so long as he does right. Hence the aphorism "St. Thomas Aquinas was the first Whig"—a pioneer of the theory of constitutional government. (The Whigs were a major British political group of the late 17th through early 19th centuries seeking to limit the royal authority and increase parliamentary power.) The society he envisages, however, is medieval, static, hierarchical, conservative, and based on limited agriculture and even more limited technology. Nonetheless, Thomism remains the most complete and lasting political doctrine of Roman Catholicism, since modified and adapted but not in principle superseded.

## DANTE

By the early 14th century the great European institutions, empire and papacy, were breaking down through mutual conflict and the emergence of national realms. But this conflict gave rise to the most complete political theory of universal and secular empire formulated in the medieval West, by the Italian poet and philosopher Dante Alighieri (1265-1321) . In *De monarchia* (*c.* 1313), still in principle highly relevant, Dante insists that only through universal peace can human faculties come to their full compass. But only "temporal monarchy" can achieve this: "a unique princedom extending over all persons in time." The aim of civilization is to actualize human potentialities and to achieve that "fullness of life which comes from the fulfillment of our being."

Monarchy, Dante argues, is necessary as a means to this end. The imperial authority of the Holy Roman emperor, moreover, comes directly from God and not through the pope. The empire is the direct heir of the Roman Empire,

*The Italian poet and philosopher Dante Alighieri.* Stock Montage/
Archive Photos/Getty Images

a legitimate authority, or Christ would not have chosen to be born under it. In subjecting the world to itself, the Roman Empire had contemplated the public good.

This high-flown argument, part of the political warfare between the partisans of the emperor and pope that was then affecting Italy, drives to essentials: that world peace can be secure only under a world authority. That Dante's argument was impractical did not concern this medieval genius, who was writing more the epitaph than the pro-spectus of the Holy Roman Empire; he was concerned, like Aquinas, to create a political philosophy with a clear-cut aim and a universal view.

Out of the grand but impractical visions of the High Middle Ages in the 13th-century climax of Christian civi-lization, there emerged by early-modern times the idea of a well-governed realm, its authority derived from the community itself, with a program designed to ensure the solvency and administrative efficiency of a secular state. In spite of the decline of the civilization of antiquity in the West, the Greco-Roman sense of purpose, of the rule of law, and of the responsibility of power survived in Christian form.

# CHAPTER 5

## Political Philosophy: From the Italian Renaissance to the End of the 18th Century

As secular authority replaced ecclesiastical authority and as the dominant interest of the age shifted from religion to politics, it was natural that the rivalries of the national states and their persistent crises of internal order should raise with renewed urgency philosophical problems, practically dormant since pre-Christian times, about the nature and the moral status of political power. This new preoccupation with national unity, internal security, state power, and international justice stimulated the growth of political philosophy in Italy, France, England, and Holland.

## NICCOLÒ MACHIAVELLI

In the thought of the Italian political philosopher Niccolò Machiavelli may be seen a complete secularization of political philosophy. Machiavelli was an experienced diplomat and administrator, and, since he stated flatly how the power struggle was conducted in Renaissance Italy, he won a shocking reputation. He was not, however, without idealism about the old Roman republic, and he admired the independent spirit of the German and Swiss cities. This idealism made him all the more disgusted with Italian politics, of which he makes a disillusioned and objective analysis. Writing in retirement after political disgrace, Machiavelli states firmly that:

> *since this is to be asserted in general of men, that they are ungrateful, fickle, false, cowards, covetous, and as long as you succeed they are yours entirely: they will offer you their blood, property, life, and children...when the need is far distant; but when it approaches they turn against you.*

And again:

> *since the desires of men are insatiable, nature prompting them to desire all things and fortune permitting them to enjoy but few, there results a constant discontent in their minds, and a loathing of what they possess.*

This view of human nature, already expressed by Plato and St. Augustine, is here unredeemed by Plato's doctrine of Forms or by St. Augustine's dogma of salvation through grace. Machiavelli accepts the facts and advises the ruler to act accordingly. The prince, he states, must combine the strength of the lion with the cunning of the fox: he must always be vigilant, ruthless, and prompt, striking down or neutralizing his adversaries without warning. And when he does an injury, it must be total. For "men ought to be either well treated or crushed, because they can avenge themselves of lighter injuries, of more serious ones they cannot." Moreover, "irresolute princes who follow a neutral path are generally ruined." He advises that it is best to come down at the right moment on the winning side and that conquered cities ought to be either governed directly by the tyrant himself residing there or destroyed. Furthermore, princes, unlike private men, need not keep faith: since politics reflects the law of the jungle, the state is a law unto itself, and normal moral rules do not apply to it.

Machiavelli had stated with unblinking realism how, in fact, tyrants behave, and, far from criticizing their conduct or distinguishing between the just prince who rules by law and the tyrant whose laws are in his own breast, he considers that the successful ruler has to be beyond morality, since the safety and expansion of the state are the supreme objective. In this myopic view, the cosmic visions of Aquinas and Dante are disregarded, and politics becomes a fight for survival. Within his terms of reference, Machiavelli made a convincing case, though as an experienced diplomat he might have realized that dependability in fact pays and that systematic deceit, treachery, and violence usually bring about their own nemesis.

## THOMAS HOBBES

The 17th-century English philosopher Thomas Hobbes, who spent his life as a tutor and companion to great noblemen, was a writer of genius with a greater power of phrase than any other English political philosopher. He was not, as he is sometimes misrepresented, a prophet of "bourgeois" individualism, advocating free competition in a capitalist free market. On the contrary, he was writing in a preindustrial, if increasingly commercial, society and did not much admire wealth as such but rather "honours." He was socially conservative and eager to give a new philosophical sanction to a hierarchical, if businesslike, commonwealth in which family authority was most important.

Philosophically, Hobbes was influenced by nominalist scholastic philosophy, which had discarded Thomist metaphysics (the metaphysics of Aquinas and his followers) and had accepted strict limitations on the powers of mind. He therefore based his conclusions on the rudimentary mathematical physics and psychology of his day and aimed at practical objectives—order and stability. He believed that the fundamental physical law of life was motion and that the predominant human impulses were fear and, among those above the poverty level, pride and vanity. Humans, Hobbes argued, are strictly conditioned and limited by these laws, and he tried to create a science of politics that would reflect them. "The skill of making, and maintaining Common-wealths," therefore:

> *consisteth in certain Rules, as doth Arithmetique and Geometry; not (as Tennis play) on Practise onely: which Rules, neither poor men have the leisure, nor men that have had the leisure, have hitherto had the curiosity, or the method to find out.*

Hobbes ignores the Classical and Thomist concepts of a transcendent law of nature, itself reflecting divine law, and of a "Great Chain of Being" whereby the universe is held harmoniously together. Following the practical method of investigation advocated by the French philosopher René Descartes, Hobbes states plainly that power creates law, not law power. For law is law only if it can be enforced, and the price of security is one supreme sovereign public power. For, without it, such is the competitive nature of humanity, that once more than subsistence has been achieved, people are actuated by vanity and ambition, and there is a war of all against all. The true law of nature is self-preservation, he argues, which can be achieved only if the citizens make a compact among themselves to transfer their individual power to the "leviathan" (ruler), who alone can preserve them in security. Such a commonwealth has no intrinsic supernatural or moral sanction: it derives its original authority from the people and can command loyalty only so long as it succeeds in keeping the peace. He thus uses both the old concepts of natural law and contract, often invoked to justify resistance to authority, as a sanction for it.

*The English philosopher Thomas Hobbes saw government mainly as a means of ensuring the collective security of its citizens.* Hulton Archive/Getty Images

Hobbes, like Machiavelli, starts from an assumption of basic human folly, competitiveness, and depravity and contradicts Aristotle's assumption that man is by nature a political animal. On the contrary, he is naturally antisocial, and, even when men meet for business and profit, only "a certain market-fellowship" is engendered. All society is only for gain or glory, and the only true equality between humans is their power to kill each other. Hobbes sees and desires no other equality. Indeed, he specifically discouraged "men of low degree from a saucy behaviour towards their betters."

The *Leviathan* (1651) horrified most of his contemporaries; Hobbes was accused of atheism and of "maligning the Human Nature." But, if his remedies were tactically impractical, in political philosophy he had gone very deep by providing the sovereign nation-state with a pragmatic justification and directing it to utilitarian ends.

## BENEDICT DE SPINOZA

The 17th-century Dutch Jewish philosopher Benedict de Spinoza also tried to make a scientific political theory, but it was more humane and more modern. Hobbes assumes a preindustrial and economically conservative society, but Spinoza assumes a more urban setting. Like Hobbes, he is Cartesian (a follower of Descartes), aiming at a scientific basis for political philosophy, but, whereas Hobbes was dogmatic and authoritarian, Spinoza desired toleration and intellectual liberty, by which alone human life achieves its highest quality. Spinoza, reacting against the ideological wars of religion and skeptical of both metaphysics and religious dogma, was a scientific humanist who justified political power solely by its usefulness. If state power breaks down and can no longer protect him or if it turns against him, frustrates, or ruins his life, then any individual is justified in resisting it, since it no longer fulfills its purpose. It has no intrinsic divine or metaphysical authority.

In the *Tractatus Theologico-Politicus* (1670) and the *Tractatus Politicus* (published posthumously in 1677), Spinoza develops this theme. He intends, he writes, "not to laugh at men or weep over them or hate them, but to understand them." In contrast to St. Augustine, he glorifies life and holds that governments should not try to "change men from rational beings into beasts or puppets, but enable them to develop their minds and bodies in security and to employ their reason unshackled." The more life is enjoyed, he declares, the more the individual participates in the divine nature. God is immanent in the entire process of nature, in which all creatures follow the laws of their own being to the limit of their powers. All are bound by their own consciousness, and humanity creates its own values.

It seems that Spinoza thought good government approximated to that of the free burgesses of Amsterdam, a city in which religious toleration and relative political liberty had been realized. He is thus a pioneer of a scientific humanist view of government and of the neutrality of the state in matters of belief.

## RICHARD HOOKER

Out of the breakup of the medieval social order, there emerged the humanist but sceptical outlook of Machiavelli and then the scientific humanist principles of Descartes, Hobbes, and Spinoza, from which the utilitarian and pragmatic outlook of modern times derives.

Another influential and politically important strain of political philosophy emerged from the Reformation and Counter-Reformation of the 16th and 17th centuries. During this period Protestant and Catholic dogmatists denounced each other and even attacked the authority of princes who, from interest or conviction, supported one side or the other. Political assassination became endemic, for both Protestant and Catholic divines declared that it was legitimate to kill a heretical ruler. Appeal was made to rival religious authority as well as to conscience. In the resulting welter Hobbes and Spinoza advocated a sovereign state as the remedy. But other political philosophers salvaged the old Thomist concept of a divine cosmic order and of natural and human laws sanctioning the state. They also put forth the Classical and medieval idea of the derivation of public power from the commonwealth as a whole and the responsibility of princes to the law. When Hobbes wrote that might makes right, he outraged such critics, who continued to assert that public power was responsible to God and the laws and that it was right to resist a tyrant who declared that the laws were in his own breast. This political theory was most influentially developed in England, where it inspired the constitutionalism that would also predominate in the United States.

Richard Hooker, an Anglican divine who wrote *Of the Lawes of Ecclesiasticall Politie* (1593–1597), reconciled Thomist doctrines of transcendent and natural law, binding on all human beings, with the authority of the Elizabethan Church of England, which he defended against the Puritan appeal to conscience. Society, he argued, is itself the fulfillment of natural law, of which human and positive law are reflections, adapted to society. Public power is not something personal, for it derives from the community under law. Thus:

> *the lawful power of making laws to command whole politic societies of men belongeth so properly unto the same entire societies, that for any prince... to exercise the same of himself...is no better than mere tyranny.*

Such power can derive either directly from God or else from the people. The prince is responsible to God and the community; he is not, like Hobbes's ruler, a law unto himself. Law makes the king, not the king law.

Hooker, indeed, insisted that "the prince has a delegated power, from the Parliament of England, together with the convocation (of clergy) annexed thereto...whereupon the very essence of all government doth depend." This is the power of the crown in parliament in a balanced constitution, hence an idea of harmonious government by consent. The Thomist medieval universal harmony had been adapted to the nation-state.

## JOHN LOCKE

It was John Locke, politically the most influential English philosopher, who further developed this doctrine. His *Two Treatises of Government* (1689) were written to justify the Glorious Revolution of 1688–1689, and his *Letter Concerning Toleration* (1689) was written with a plain and easy urbanity, in contrast to the baroque eloquence of Hobbes. Locke was a scholar, physician, and man of affairs, well-experienced in politics and business. As a philosopher he accepted strict limitations on the faculties of the mind, and his political philosophy is moderate and sensible, aimed at a balance of power between the executive, the judiciary, and the legislature, though with a bias toward the last.

*The English political philosopher John Locke viewed the authority of government as deriving from a social contract between government and its citizens.* Stock Montage/Archive Photos/ Getty Images

His first *Treatise* was devoted to confuting the royalist doctrine of the divine right of kings by descent from Adam, an argument then taken very seriously and reflecting the idea of government as an aspect of the divinely ordained Great Chain of Being. If this order were broken, chaos would ensue. The argument was part of the contemporary conflict of the Ancients and the Moderns.

Locke tried to provide an answer by defining a limited purpose for political power, which purpose he considered to be "a right of making laws with penalties of death, and consequently all less penalties, for the regulating and preserving of property, and of employing the force of the community in execution of such laws, and in the defense of the commonwealth from foreign injury, and all this only for the public good." The authority of government derives from a contract between the rulers and the people, and the contract binds both parties. It is thus a limited power, proceeding according to established laws and "directed to no other end but the peace, safety, and public good of the people."

Whatever its form, government, to be legitimate, must govern by "declared and reasoned laws," and, since every individual has a "property" in his own person and has "mixed his labour" with what he owns, government has no right to take it from him without his consent. It was the threat of attack on the laws, property, and the Protestant religion that had roused resistance to the Roman Catholic monarch James II. Locke is expressing the concerns and interests of the landed and moneyed men by whose consent James's successor, William III, came to the throne, and his commonwealth is strictly conservative, limiting the franchise and the preponderant power to the propertied classes (and to men, of course). Locke was thus no democrat in the modern sense and was much concerned to make the poor work harder. Like Hooker, he assumes a conservative social hierarchy with a relatively weak executive power and defends the propertied classes both against a ruler by divine right and against radicals. In advocating toleration in religion, he was more liberal: freedom of conscience, like property, he argued, is a natural right of all men. Within the possibilities of the time, Locke thus advocated a constitutional mixed government, limited by parliamentary control of the armed forces and of supply. Designed mainly to protect the rights of property, it was deprived of the right of arbitrary taxation or imprisonment without trial and was in theory responsible to all the people through the politically conscious minority who were thought to represent them.

Although Locke was socially conservative, his writings are very important in the rise of liberalism in political philosophy. He vindicates the responsibility of government to the governed, the rule of law through impartial judges, and the toleration of religious and speculative opinion. He is an enemy of the totalitarian state, drawing on medieval arguments and deploying them in practical, modern terms.

## EDMUND BURKE

The 18th-century British statesman Edmund Burke (1729-1797), while elaborating Whig constitutional doctrine expressed with such common sense by Locke, wrote with more emotion and took more account of time and tradition. While reiterating that government is responsible to the governed and distinguishing between a political society and a mere mob, he thought that governments were trustees for previous generations and for posterity.

He made the predominant political philosophy of the 18th-century establishment appear more attractive and moral, but he wrote no great single work of political philosophy, expressing himself instead in numerous pamphlets and speeches.

In his early *A Vindication of Natural Society* (1756), Burke is critical of the sufferings imposed by government, but his "Thoughts on the Cause of the Present Discontents" defines and defends the principles of the Whig establishment. He invoked a transcendent morality to sanction a constitutional commonwealth, but he detested abstract political theories in whose name society is likely to be vivisected. He set great store by ordered liberty and denounced the arbitrary power of the Jacobins who had captured the French Revolution. In his *Reflections on the Revolution in France* (1790) and *An Appeal from the New to the Old Whigs* (1791), he discerned in the doctrine of sovereignty of the people, in whose name the revolutionaries were destroying the old order, another and worse form of arbitrary power. No single generation has the right to destroy the agreed and inherited fabric of society, and "neither the few nor the many have the right to govern by their will." A country is not a mere physical locality, he argued, but a community in time into which people are born, and only within the existing constitution and by the consent of its representatives can changes legitimately be made. Once the frame of society has been smashed and its law violated, the people become a "mere multitude told by the head," at the mercy of any dictator who can seize power. He was realistic in predicting the consequences of violent revolution, which usually ends up in some kind of dictatorship. Burke, in sophisticated accents, spoke for the ancient and worldwide rule of custom and conservatism and supplied a needed romanticism to the calculating good sense of Locke.

# JACOBIN CLUB

The Jacobin Club, also called the Jacobins, was the most famous political group of the French Revolution. Identified with extreme egalitarianism and violence, it led the Revolutionary government from mid-1793 to mid-1794.

The Jacobins originated as the Club Breton at Versailles, where the deputies from Brittany to the Estates-General (later the National Assembly) of 1789 met with deputies from other parts of France to concert their action. It was reconstituted, probably in December 1789, after the National Assembly moved to Paris, under the name of Society of the Friends of the Constitution, but it was commonly called the Jacobin Club because its sessions were held in a former convent of the Dominicans, who were known in

*A meeting of the Jacobins, an egalitarian political group that flourished during the French Revolution.* Hulton Archive/Getty Images

Paris as Jacobins. Its purpose was to protect the gains of the Revolution against a possible aristocratic reaction. The club soon admitted nondeputies and acquired affiliates throughout France.

After the overthrow of the monarchy, in August 1792 (in which the Jacobin Club did not have a direct role), the club entered a new phase as one of the major groups directing the Revolution. It acquired a democratic character with the admission of the leftist Montagnard deputies in the National Convention (the new legislature) and also a more popular one as it responded to the demands of the Parisian working and artisan class. Through the early phase of the Convention, the club was a meeting place for the Montagnards, and it agitated for the execution of the king (January 1793) and for the overthrow of the moderate Girondins (June 1793).

With the establishment of the Revolutionary dictatorship, beginning in the summer of 1793, the local Jacobin clubs became instruments of the Reign of Terror. The clubs, as part of the administrative machinery of government, raised supplies for the army and policed local markets. They also watched over people whose opinions were suspect, led the dechristianizing movement, and organized Revolutionary festivals.

The Parisian club was increasingly associated with the Jacobin leader Maximilien de Robespierre, who dominated the Revolutionary government through his position on the Committee of Public Safety. After the fall of Robespierre on July 27, 1794, the Parisian club was temporarily closed. It reopened as a centre of opposition to the government but it was permanently closed on Nov. 11, 1794.

The name Jacobin was also applied to radicals in England and other countries in the period of the French Revolution.

# GIAMBATTISTA VICO

The political philosophies hitherto surveyed contained little idea of progress. In antiquity the idea of cyclic recurrence predominated, and even 18th-century Christians believed that the world had been created in 4004 BCE and would end in the Second Coming of Christ. The 14th-century Arab philosopher of history Ibn Khaldūn had pioneered a vast sociological view of the historical process, but in western Europe it was a neglected Neapolitan philosopher, Giambattista Vico, who first interpreted the past in terms of the changing consciousness of humankind. His *Scienza nuova* (1725; *New Science*) interpreted history as an organic process involving language, literature, and religion and attempted to reveal the mentality or ethos of earlier ages: the age of the gods, the heroic age, and the human age, its climax and decadence. These ages recur, and each is distinguished by mythology, heroic poetry, and rational speculation, respectively. In contrast to the legalistic, contractual, and static political philosophies then prevalent, Vico had discerned new horizons.

# MONTESQUIEU

This sort of vision was developed and elegantly popularized by the cosmopolitan French savant Montesquieu, whose work *De l'esprit des loix* (1748; *The Spirit of Laws*) won immense influence. It was an ambitious treatise on human institutions and a pioneer work of anthropology and sociology. Believing in an ordered universe—for "how could blind fate have produced intelligent beings?"—Montesquieu examined the varieties of natural law, varying customs, laws, and civilizations in different environments. He made the pedestrian good sense of Locke seem provincial, though he admired him and the British constitution. Unfortunately, he over-emphasized the separation of executive, judicial, and legislative powers, considerable in Locke's day but by his own time tending to be concentrated in the sovereignty of Parliament. This doctrine much influenced the founders of the United States and the early French Revolutionaries.

## JEAN-JACQUES ROUSSEAU

The revolutionary romanticism of the Swiss-French philosopher Jean-Jacques Rousseau may be interpreted in part as a reaction to the analytic rationalism of the Enlightenment. He was trying to escape the aridity of a purely empirical and utilitarian outlook and attempting to create a substitute for revealed religion. Rousseau's _Émile_ (1762) and _Du contrat social_ (1762; _The Social Contract_) proved revolutionary documents, and his posthumous _Considérations sur le gouvernement de Pologne_ (1782; _Considerations on the Government of Poland_) contains desultory but often valuable reflections on specific problems.

There had been radical political slogans coined in medieval peasant revolts and in the 17th century, as in the debates following the revolt of radical officers in the Cromwellian army (1647), but the inspiration of these movements had been religion. Now Rousseau proclaimed a secular egalitarianism and a romantic cult of the common man. His famous declaration "Man is born free, and everywhere he is in chains" called into question the traditional social hierarchy: hitherto, political philosophers had thought in terms of elites, but now the mass of the people had found a champion and were becoming politically conscious.

Rousseau was a romantic, given to weeping under the willows on Lake Geneva, and his political works are hypnotically readable, flaming protests by one who found the hard rationality of the 18th century too exacting. But the individual is not, as Rousseau claims, born free. He is born into society, which imposes restraints on him. Casting about to reconcile his artificial antithesis between the individual's purported natural state of freedom and his condition in society, Rousseau utilizes the old theories of contract and transforms them into the concept of the "general will." This general will, a moral will that aims at the common good and in which all participate directly, reconciles the individual and the community by representing the will of the community as deriving from the will of moral individuals, so to obey the laws of such a community is in a sense to follow one's own will, assuming that one is a moral individual.

Ideas similar to that of the general will became accepted as a basis for both the social-democratic welfare state and totalitarian dictatorships. And, since the idea was misapplied from small village or civic communities to great sovereign nation-states, Rousseau was also the prophet of a nationalism that he never advocated. Rousseau himself wanted a federal Europe. He never wrote the proposed sequel to the *The Social Contract*, in which he meant to deal with international politics, but he declared that existing governments lived in a state of nature, that their obsession with conquest was imbecilic, and that "if we could realize a European republic for one day, it would be enough to make it last for ever." But, with a flash of realism, he thinks the project impracticable, because of human folly.

That the concept of general will was vague only increased its adaptability and prestige: it would both make constitutionalism more liberal and dynamic and give demagogues and dictators the excuse for "forcing people to be free" (that is, forcing people to follow the general will, as interpreted by the ruling forces). Rousseau could inspire liberals, such as the 19th-century English philosopher T.H. Green, to a creative view of a state helping people to make the best of their potential through a variety of free institutions. It could also play into the hands of demagogues claiming to represent the general will and bent on molding society according to their own abstractions.

# CHAPTER 6

## Political Philosophy: The 19th Century

Political philosophy in the 19th century was influenced by several changes in European and American intellectual culture and society. Chief among them were the Romantic movement of the early 19th century, which was a poetic revolt against reason in favour of feeling; the maturation of the Industrial Revolution, which caused untold misery as well as prosperity and prompted a multitude of philosophies of social reform; and the revolutions of 1848 in Paris, Germany, and Vienna, which reflected stark class divisions and first implanted in the European consciousness the concepts of the bourgeoisie and the proletariat.

Romanticism influenced both German idealists and philosophers of irrationalism. And experiences of economic discord and social unrest produced the ameliorative social philosophy of English utilitarianism and the revolutionary doctrines of Karl Marx.

## UTILITARIANISM

A major force in the political and social thought of the 19th century was utilitarianism, the doctrine that the actions of governments should be judged simply by the extent to which they promoted the "greatest happiness of the greatest number." The founder of the utilitarian school was Jeremy Bentham, an eccentric Englishman trained in the law. Bentham judged all laws and institutions by their utility thus defined. "The Fabric of Felicity," he wrote, "must be reared by the hands of reason and Law."

Artist's depiction of a day-labourers' uprising being broken up by the National Guard in Vienna, 1848. Uprisings such as this brought into stark relief the division between the proletariat and the upper classes. Imagno/Hulton Archive/Getty Images

Bentham's *Fragment, on Government* (1776) and *Introduction to the Principles of Morals and Legislation* (1789) elaborated a utilitarian political philosophy. Bentham was an atheist and an exponent of the new laissez-faire economics of Adam Smith and David Ricardo, but he inspired the spate of legislation that, after the Reform Bill of 1832, had tackled the worst consequences of 18th-century inefficiency and of the Industrial Revolution. His influence, moreover, spread widely abroad. At first a simple reformer of law, Bentham attacked notions of contract and natural law as superfluous. "The indestructible prerogatives of mankind," he wrote, "have no need to be supported upon the sandy foundation of a fiction." The justification of government is pragmatic, its aim improvement and the release of the free choice of individuals and the play of market forces that will create prosperity. Bentham thought people far more reasonable and calculating than they are and brushed aside all the Christian and humanist ideas rationalizing instinctive loyalty and awe. He thought society could advance by calculation of pleasure and pain, and his *Introduction* even tries to work out "the value of a lot of pleasure and pain, how now to be measured." He compared the relative gratifications of health, wealth, power, friendship, and benevolence, as well as those of "irascible appetite" and "antipathy." He also thought of punishment purely as a deterrent, not as retribution, and graded offenses on the harm they did to happiness, not on how much they offended God or tradition.

If Bentham's psychology was naïve, that of his disciple James Mill was philistine. Mill postulated an economic individual whose decisions, if freely taken, would always be in his own interest, and he believed that universal suffrage, along with utilitarian legislation by a sovereign parliament, would produce the kind of happiness and well-being that Bentham desired. In his *Essay on Government* (1828) Mill thus shows a doctrinaire faith in a literate electorate as the means to good government and in laissez-faire economics as a means to social harmony.

This utilitarian tradition was humanized by James Mill's son, John Stuart Mill, one of the most influential of mid-Victorian liberals. Whereas James Mill had been entirely pragmatic, his son tried to enhance more sophisticated values. He thought that civilization depended on a tiny minority of creative minds and on the free play of speculative intelligence. He detested conventional public opinion and feared that complete democracy, far from emancipating opinion, would make it more restrictive. Amid the dogmatic and strident voices of mid-19th-century nationalists, utopians, and revolutionaries, the quiet, if sometimes priggish, voice of mid-Victorian liberalism proved extremely influential in the ruling circles of Victorian England.

Accepting democracy as inevitable, John Stuart Mill expressed the still optimistic and progressive views of an intellectual elite. Without complete liberty of opinion, he insisted, civilizations ossify. The quality of progress results not merely from the blind forces of economic competition but from the free play of mind. The worth of the state in the long run is only the worth of the individuals composing it, and without people of genius society would become a "stagnant pool." This militant humanist, unlike his father, was aware of the dangers of even benevolent bureaucratic power and declared that a state that "dwarfs its men" is culturally insignificant.

Mill also advocated the legal and social emancipation of women, holding that ability was wasted by mid-Victorian conventions. He believed that the masses could be educated into accepting the values of liberal civilization, but he defended private property and was as wary of rapid extensions of the franchise as of bureaucratic power.

## ALEXIS DE TOCQUEVILLE

Mill's friend Alexis de Tocqueville, whose *De la démocratie en Amérique* (*Democracy in America*) appeared in 1835–1840, was a French civil servant who was concerned with maintaining the standards and creativeness of civilization in the face of mass democracy. Since the United States was then the only existing large-scale democracy,

Tocqueville decided to study it firsthand, and the result was a classic account of early 19th-century American civilization. "We cannot," he wrote, "prevent the conditions of men from becoming equal, but it depends upon ourselves whether the principle of equality will lead them to servitude or freedom, to knowledge or barbarism, to prosperity or wretchedness." He feared the possible abuse of power by centralized government, unrestrained by the old privileged classes, and thought it essential to "educate democracy" so that, although it would never have the "wild virtues" of the old regimes, it would have its own dignity, good sense, and even benevolence. Tocqueville greatly admired American representative institutions and made a penetrating analysis of the new power of the press. He realized, as few people then did, that the United States and Russia would become world powers, and he contrasted the freedom of the one and the despotism of the other. He also foresaw that under democracy education would be respected more as a ladder to success than for its intrinsic content and might thus become mediocre. He was alive to the dangers of uniform mediocrity but believed, like Mill, that democracy could be permeated by creative ideas.

## T.H. GREEN

This kind of humanism was given a more elaborate philosophical content by the English philosopher T.H. Green, whose *Lectures on the Principles of Political Obligation* (1885) greatly influenced members of the Liberal Party in the British governments of the period 1906–1915. Green, like John Stuart Mill and Tocqueville, wished to extend the minority culture to the people and even to use state power to "hinder hindrances to the good life." He had absorbed from Aristotle, Spinoza, Rousseau, and the German idealist philosopher G.W.F. Hegel an organic theory of the state. The latter, by promoting the free play of spontaneous institutions, ought to help individuals to "secure the common good of society [and] enable them to make the best of themselves."

While hostile to the abuse of landed property, Green did not advocate socialism. He accepted the idea that property should be private and unequally distributed and thought the operation of the free market the best way to benefit the whole of society; for free trade would, he thought, diminish the inequalities of wealth in a common prosperity. But Green would have extended the power of the state over education, health, housing, town planning, and the relief of unemployment—a new departure in Liberal thought. These recommendations are embedded in the most elaborate and close-knit intellectual construction made by any modern British political philosopher, and they laid the foundation of the British welfare state.

## LIBERAL NATIONALISM

Whereas Green avoided the extension of liberal and constitutional principles into international affairs, the Italian patriot and revolutionary prophet Giuseppe Mazzini made it his vision and became the most influential prophet of liberal nationalism. He envisaged a harmony of free peoples—a "sisterhood of nations"—in which the rule of military empires would be thrown off, the destruction of clerical and feudal privileges accomplished, and the emancipated peoples regenerated by

*Piedmontese troops attack Madonna della Scoperta in northern Italy during the Battle of Solferino. The battle was the last engagement during the Risorgimento, which culminated in Italian unification.* Hulton Archive/Getty Images

means of education and universal suffrage. This vision inspired the more idealistic aspects of the Italian Risorgimento (national revival or resurrection) and of nationalistic revolts in Europe and beyond. Although, in fact, fervid nationalism often proved destructive, Mazzini advocated a united Europe of free peoples, in which national singularities would be transcended in a pan-European harmony. This sort of liberal democratic idealism was catching, and even if it frequently inspired Machiavellian policies, it also inspired Pres. Woodrow Wilson of the United States—who, had he not been thwarted by domestic opposition—might well have made the Mazzini-inspired League of Nations a success. Moreover, the modern European Union owes much to the apparently impractical liberal idealism of Mazzini.

# RISORGIMENTO

The Risorgimento (Italian: "Rising Again") was a 19th-century movement for Italian unification that culminated in the establishment of the Kingdom of Italy in 1861. It was an ideological and literary movement that helped to arouse the national consciousness of the Italian people, and it led to a series of political events that freed the Italian states from foreign domination and united them politically. Although the Risorgimento has attained the status of a national myth, its essential meaning remains a controversial question. The classic interpretation (expressed in the writings of the philosopher Benedetto Croce) sees the Risorgimento as the triumph of liberalism, but more recent views criticize it as an aristocratic and bourgeois revolution that failed to include the masses.

The main impetus to the Risorgimento came from reforms introduced by the French when they dominated Italy during the period of the French Revolutionary and Napoleonic wars (1796–1815). A number of Italian states were briefly consolidated, first as republics and then as satellite states of the French empire; even more importantly, the Italian middle class grew in numbers and was allowed to participate in government.

After Napoleon's defeat in 1815, the Italian states were restored to their former rulers. Under the domination of Austria, these states took on a conservative character. Secret societies such as the Carbonari opposed this development in the 1820s and '30s. The first avowedly republican and national group was Young Italy, founded by Giuseppe Mazzini in 1831. This society, which represented the democratic aspect of the Risorgimento, hoped to educate the Italian people to a sense of their nationhood and to encourage the masses to rise against the existing reactionary regimes. Other groups, such as the Neo-Guelfs, envisioned an Italian confederation headed by the pope; still others favoured unification under the house of Savoy, monarchs of the liberal northern Italian state of Piedmont-Sardinia.

After the failure of liberal and republican revolutions in 1848, leadership passed to Piedmont. With French help, the Piedmontese defeated the Austrians in 1859 and united most of Italy under their rule by 1861. The annexation of Venetia in 1866 and papal Rome in 1870 marked the final unification of Italy and hence the end of the Risorgimento.

## AMERICAN CONSTITUTIONALISM

The founders of the United States were deeply influenced by republicanism, by Locke, and by the optimism of the European Enlightenment. George Washington, John Adams, and Thomas Jefferson all concurred that laws, rather than men, should be the final sanction and that government should be responsible to the governed. But the influence of Locke and the Enlightenment was not entirely happy. Adams, who followed Washington as president, prescribed a constitution with a balance of executive and legislative power checked by an independent judiciary. The federal constitution, moreover, could be amended only by a unanimous vote of the states. Eager to safeguard state liberties and the rights of property, the founding fathers gave the federal government insufficient revenues and coercive powers, as a result of which the constitution was stigmatized as being "no more than a Treaty of Alliance." Yet the federal union was preserved. The civil power controlled the military, and there was religious toleration and freedom of the press and of economic enterprise. Most significantly, the concept of natural rights had found expression in the Declaration of Independence (1776) and was to influence markedly political and legal developments in the ensuing decades, as well as inspire the French Declaration of the Rights of Man and of the Citizen (1789).

Painting depicting the signing of the U.S. Constitution in 1787. A system of checks and balances was specifically incorporated into the country's constitution by the founding fathers. MPI/Archive Photos/Getty Images

## ANARCHISM AND UTOPIANISM

While a liberal political philosophy within a framework of capitalistic free trade and constitutional self-government dominated the greatest Western powers, mounting criticism developed against centralized government itself. Radical utopianism and anarchism, previously expounded mainly by religious sects, became secularized in works such as *Political Justice* (1793) by William Godwin, *New View of Society* (1813) by Robert Owen, and voluminous anticlerical writings by Pierre-Joseph Proudhon.

The English philosopher William Godwin, an extreme individualist, shared Bentham's confidence in the reasonableness of humankind. He denounced the wars accepted by most political philosophers and all centralized coercive states. The tyranny of demagogues and of "multitudes drunk with power" he regarded as being as bad as that of kings and oligarchs. The remedy, he thought, was not violent revolution, which produces tyranny, but education and freedom, including sexual freedom. His was a program of high-minded atheistic anarchy.

The English socialist Robert Owen, a cotton spinner who had made a fortune, also insisted that bad institutions, not original sin or intrinsic folly, caused the evils of society, and he sought to remedy them by changing the economic and educational system. He thus devised a scheme of model cooperative communities that would increase production, permit humane education, and release the naturally benevolent qualities of humankind.

The French moralist and advocate of social reform Pierre-Joseph Proudhon attacked the "tentacular" nation-state and aimed at a classless society in which major capitalism would be abolished. Self-governing producers, no longer slaves of bureaucrats and capitalists, would permit the realization of an intrinsic human dignity, and federation would replace the accepted condition of war between sovereign states. Proudhon tried to transform society by rousing the mass of the people to cooperative humanitarian consciousness.

## HENRI DE SAINT-SIMON AND AUGUSTE COMTE

Another revolt against the prevalent establishment, national and international, was made by the French social philosopher Henri de Saint-Simon, who wanted to develop the Industrial Revolution so as to ameliorate the condition of the poorest classes.

This would be achieved not through political revolution but through a government of bankers and administrators who would supersede kings, aristocrats, and politicians. If

France were suddenly deprived of 3,000 leading scientists, engineers, bankers, painters, poets, and writers, he argued, the result would be catastrophic, but if all the courtiers and bishops and 10,000 landowners vanished, the loss, though deplorable, would be much less severe. Saint-Simon also demanded a united Europe, superseding the warring nation-states, with a European parliament and a joint development of industry and communication. He also invented a synthetic religion appropriate to a scientific phase of history, with a cult of Isaac Newton and the great figures of science.

Saint-Simon's disciple Auguste Comte went further. His *Cours de philosophie positive* (1830–1842; *Course of Positive Philosophy*) and *Système de politique positive*, 4 vol. (1851–1854; *System of Positive Polity*), elaborated a "religion of humanity," with ritual, calendar, a priesthood of scientists, and secular saints, including Julius Caesar, Dante, and Joan of Arc. Society would be ruled by bankers and technocrats and Europe united into a Western republic. This doctrine, backed by pioneering

A colourized engraving of a portrait of French philosopher Auguste Comte by Tony Toullion. Comte proposed a political philosophy in keeping with modern industrial society of the 19th century. Apic/Hulton Archive/Getty Images

sociology, won much influence among intellectuals. Comte, like Saint-Simon, tackled the essential questions: how to deploy the power of modern technology for the benefit of all humankind; how to avoid wars between sovereign states; and how to fill the void left by the waning of Christian beliefs.

# G.W.F. HEGEL

Whereas the utopian reformers had discarded metaphysical arguments, the German idealist philosopher G.W.F. Hegel claimed to apprehend the totality of the cosmos by speculative cognition. Like Vico, he saw the past in terms of changing consciousness, but he viewed the historical process as one of "becoming" rather than as one of eternal recurrence. Hegel had no adequate historical data for his intuitions, since the whole of world history was less known then than it is today, but his novel sweep and range of theory proved an intoxicating substitute for religion. He divided world history into four epochs: the patriarchal Eastern empire, the brilliant Greek boyhood, the severe manhood of Rome, and the Germanic phase after the Reformation. The "Absolute," like a conductor, summons each people to their finest hour, and neither individuals nor states have any rights against them during their historically determined period of supremacy. Many felt some sense of anticlimax, however, when he claimed that the Prussian state of his own day embodied the hitherto highest self-realization of the Absolute. Not since St. Augustine had so compelling a drama been adumbrated. Hegel's drama, moreover, culminates in this world, for "the state is the divine idea as it exists on Earth."

# KARL MARX AND FRIEDRICH ENGELS

Hegel was a conservative, but his influence on the revolutionaries Karl Marx and his collaborator Friedrich Engels was profound. They inherited the Hegelian claim to understand the "totality" of history and life as it progressed through a dialectic of thesis, antithesis, and synthesis. But, whereas Hegel envisaged a conflict of nation-states, Marx and Engels thought that the dynamism of history was generated by inevitable class conflict economically determined. This was an idea even more dynamic than Hegel's and more relevant to the social upheavals that were a consequence of the Industrial Revolution. Marx was a formidable prophet whose writings prophesied an apocalypse and redemption. He was a deeply learned humanist, and his ideal was the fullest development of the human personality. But, whereas Plato was concerned with an elite, Marx cared passionately for the elevation of whole peoples.

The Marxist credo was all the more effective as it expressed with eloquent ferocity the grievances of the poor while predicting retribution and a happy ending. For the state, once captured by the class-conscious vanguard of the proletariat, would take over the means of production from the capitalists, and a brief "dictatorship of the proletariat" would establish genuine communism. The state would wither away, and individuals would at last become "fully human" in a classless society.

The powerful slogans of Marx and Engels were a natural result of the unbridled capitalism of laissez-faire, but politically they were naïve. In Classical, medieval, and humanistic political philosophy, the essential problem is the control of power, and to imagine that

*Karl Marx.* Courtesy of the trustees of the British Museum; photograph, J.R. Freeman & Co. Ltd.

a dictatorship, once established, will wither away is utopian. As the Russian anarchist Mikhail Bakunin observed:

> *The revolutionary dictatorship of the doctrinaires who put science before life would differ from the established state only in external trappings. The substance of both are a tyranny of the minority over the majority—in the name of the many and the supreme wisdom of the few.*

The revolutionaries would vivisect society in the name of dogmas and "destroy the present order, only to erect their own rigid dictatorship among its ruins."

# CHAPTER 7

## Political Philosophy: From the 20th Century to the Present

Nineteenth-century European civilization had been the first to dominate and pervade the whole world and to create a new self-sustaining productivity in which all eventually might share. But, as Saint-Simon had pointed out, this civilization had a fatal flaw. The rule of law, accepted within the politically advanced states, had never been achieved among them. Heavily armed nations and empires remained in a Hobbesian "posture of war," and Classical and medieval ideals of world order had long been discarded. Within states, also, laissez-faire capitalism had exacerbated class conflicts, while the decline of religious belief had undermined traditional solidarity. And in 1914, when a general European war broke out, the peoples, contrary to the hopes of cosmopolitan revolutionaries, rallied behind their national governments. When the victorious powers (mainly France, Great Britain, Russia, Italy, Japan, and, from 1917, the United States) failed to promote world order through the League of Nations, a second global conflict, even more horrific than the first, ensued, during which were developed weapons (atomic bombs) so destructive as to threaten life everywhere.

In the aftermath of these catastrophes and the worldwide revulsion they occasioned, not least against the European colonial powers, various mainstreams of political philosophy may be discerned. First, Marxism continued to inspire revolutionary doctrines as well as more-sober political and cultural analyses, some relying on insights borrowed from psychoanalytic theory. Second, liberalism continued to be developed and refined, partly in response to libertarian and communitarian critiques. Third, a line of thought pursued by Michel Foucault and later postmodern philosophers questioned the possibility of objectively valid political values and genuinely neutral political institutions. Fourth, some feminist philosophers applied concepts from liberal and Marxist political theory to the analysis of the subordinate place of women in modern political and economic life, while a more radical school of feminists argued that the historical domination of men over women reflects the inherently oppressive nature of heterosexual relationships. And fifth, as the new century dawned, so did an increased concern about concept of "global justice" among philosophers of politics such as Nobel Prize winning economist Amartya Sen.

## MARXIST DOCTRINES

Although many of Marx's original insights into socioeconomic processes and their effects on conventional political ideology and culture are now widely accepted, his specific historical prophecies were not fulfilled. The major proletarian revolutions, for example, came not in economically advanced countries but in economically underdeveloped ones (Russia and China), and the supposedly proletarian dictatorships they produced, far from withering away or being diminished by inexorable economic trends, became even more powerful and oppressive than the governments they replaced. Soviet and eastern European communism eventually collapsed

Citizens demonstrating in Petrograd, during the Russian Revolution of 1917. The revolution was due in part to the poor performance of the Russian military during World War I. AFP/Getty Images

in failure in 1989–1991, to be replaced in Russia by a quasi-democratic capitalist oligarchy.

## VLADIMIR ILICH LENIN

The first and by far the most significant interpretation of Marx's doctrine was realized in the Soviet Union by Vladimir Ilich Lenin and developed by Joseph Stalin and was entirely authoritarian. According to Marx and Engels, the revolution could occur in Russia only after the bourgeois phase of production had "contradicted" the tsarist order. To Marx, the bourgeoisie was the social order that is dominated by the so-called middle class. The term *bourgeois* arose in medieval France, but its overtones became important in the 18th century, when the middle class of professionals, manufacturers, and their literary and political allies began to demand an influence in politics consistent with their economic status. Marx was one of many thinkers who treated the French Revolution as a revolution of the bourgeois.

In Marxist theory, the bourgeoisie plays a heroic role by revolutionizing industry and modernizing society. However, it also seeks to monopolize the benefits of this modernization by exploiting the propertyless proletariat. The end result, according to Marx, will be a final revolution in which the property of the bourgeoisie is expropriated and class conflict, exploitation, and the state are abolished.

Lenin was not willing to wait for the bourgeois phase of production to end in conflict with Russia's powerful royalty, however. He was determined to take advantage of the opportunities provided by the upheaval of World War I to settle accounts directly with the "accursed heritage of serfdom," which had survived in Russia for centuries, long after it had disappeared from the rest of Europe. In the Russian Revolution of 1917, he engineered a coup that secured the support of the peasantry and the industrial workers. He also adopted the revolutionary theorist Leon Trotsky's idea of a "permanent revolution" led from above by a small revolutionary elite.

Already in *What Is to Be Done?* (1902), Lenin had argued that an educated elite had to direct the proletarian revolution, and, when he came to power, he dissolved the constituent assembly and ruled through a "revolutionary and democratic dictatorship supported by the state power of the armed workers." In asserting the need for an elite of professional revolutionaries to seize power, Lenin reverted to Marx's program in *The Communist Manifesto* (1848) rather than conforming to the fated pattern of economic development worked out in *Das Kapital*, 3 vol. (1867, 1885, 1894).

In 1921 he further adapted theory to the times. His New Economic Policy sanctioned the development of a class of prosperous peasants, called kulaks, to keep the economy viable. For Lenin always thought in terms of world revolution, and, in spite of the failure of the Marxists in central Europe and the defeat of the Red armies in Poland, he died in the expectation of a global sequel. Thus, in *Imperialism, the Highest Stage of Capitalism* (1917), he had extended the class war into an inevitable conflict between European imperialism and the colonial peoples involved. He had been influenced by the English historian J.A. Hobson's *Imperialism, a Study* (1902), which alleged that decadent capitalism was bound to turn from glutted markets at home to exploit the toil of "reluctant and unassimilated peoples."

But, as observed by Classical, medieval, and modern constitutionalist political philosophers, authoritarian regimes suffer the tensions of all autocracies, or government in which one person possesses unlimited power. Marx himself might have thought that such planned autocracies had made the worst of his revelation.

## GYÖRGY LUKÁCS AND ANTONIO GRAMSCI

Many Marxist revisionists tended toward anarchism, stressing the Hegelian and utopian elements of Marx's theory. The Hungarian philosopher György Lukács, for example, and the German-born American philosopher Herbert Marcuse, who fled Nazi Germany in 1934, won some following in the mid-20th century among those in revolt against both authoritarian "peoples' democracies" and the diffused capitalism and meritocracy of the managerial welfare state. Lukács's *Geschichte und Klassenbewusstsein* (1923; *History and Class Consciousness*), a neo-Hegelian work, claims that only the intuition of the proletariat can properly apprehend the totality of history. But world revolution is contingent, not inevitable, and Marxism is an instrument, not a prediction. Lukács renounced this heresy after residence in the Soviet Union under Stalin, but he maintained influence through literary and dramatic criticism. After Khrushchev's denunciation of Stalin in 1956, Lukács advocated peaceful coexistence and intellectual rather than political subversion. In *Wider den missverstandenen Realismus* (1963; *The Meaning of Contemporary Realism*), he again relates Marx to Hegel and even to Aristotle, against the Stalinist claim that Marx made a radically new departure. Lukács's neo-Marxist literary criticism can be tendentious, but his neo-Hegelian insights, strikingly expressed, have appealed to those eager to salvage the more humane aspects of Marxism and to promote revolution, even against a modified capitalism and social democracy, by intellectual rather than political means.

The Italian communist philosopher Antonio Gramsci deployed a vivid rhetorical talent in attacking existing society. Gramsci was alarmed that the proletariat was being assimilated by the capitalist order. He took his stand on the already obsolescent Marxist doctrine of irreconcilable class war between bourgeois and proletariat. He aimed to unmask the bourgeois idea of liberty and to replace parliaments by an "implacable machine" of workers' councils, which would destroy the current social order through a dictatorship of the proletariat. "Democracy," he wrote, "is our worst enemy. We must be ready to fight it because it blurs the clear separation of classes."

Not only would parliamentary democracy and established law be unmasked, but culture, too, would be transformed. A workers' civilization, with its great industry, large cities, and "tumultuous and intense life," would create a new civilization with new poetry, art, drama, fashions, and language. Gramsci insisted that the old culture should be destroyed and that education should be wrenched from the grip of the ruling classes and the church.

But this militant revolutionary was also a utopian. He turned bitterly hostile to Stalin's regime, for he believed, like Engels, that the dictatorship of the workers' state would wither away. "We do not wish," he wrote, "to freeze the dictatorship." Following world revolution, a classless society would emerge, and humankind would be free to master nature instead of being involved in a class war. Gramsci was arrested by the Fascist government of Benito Mussolini in 1926 and spent the next 11 years in prison; he died shortly after his release for medical care in 1937.

## CRITICAL THEORY

Critical theory, a broad-based Marxist-oriented approach to the study of society, was first developed in the 1920s by the philosophers Max Horkheimer, Theodor Adorno, and Herbert Marcuse at the Institute for Social Research in Frankfurt, Ger. They and other members of the Frankfurt School, as this group came to be called, fled Germany after the Nazis came to power in 1933. The institute was relocated to Columbia University in the United States and remained there until 1949, when it was reestablished in Frankfurt. The most prominent representatives of the Frankfurt School and of critical theory from the mid-20th century were Marcuse and Jürgen Habermas.

The question initially addressed by critical theorists was why the working classes in advanced capitalist countries were generally unmotivated to press for radical social change in their own interests. They attempted to develop a theory of capitalist social relations and to analyze the various forms of cultural and ideological oppression arising from them. They also undertook major studies of fascism and later of dictatorial communist regimes. After World War II, during the era of the Cold War, critical theorists viewed the world as divided between two inherently oppressive models of social development. In these historical circumstances, questions concerning human liberation—what it consists of and how it can be attained—seemed especially urgent.

## MAX HORKHEIMER, THEODOR ADORNO, AND HERBERT MARCUSE

In *Dialectic of Enlightenment* (1947), Horkheimer and Adorno argued that the celebration of reason by thinkers of the 18th-century Enlightenment had led to the development of technologically sophisticated but oppressive and inhumane modes of governance, exemplified in the 20th century by fascism and totalitarianism. In works published in the 1950s and '60s, Marcuse attacked both the ideological conformism of managerial capitalism and the bureaucratic oppression of the communist "peoples' democracies." In his best-known and most influential work, *One-Dimensional Man: Studies in the Ideology of Advanced Industrial Society* (1964), he argued that the modern capitalist "affluent" society oppresses even those who are successful within it while maintaining their complacency through the ersatz satisfactions of consumer culture. By cultivating such shallow forms of experience and by blocking critical understanding of the real workings of the system, the affluent society condemns its members to a "one-dimensional" existence of intellectual and spiritual poverty. In later works, seeing human freedom as everywhere in retreat, Marcuse transferred the redeeming mission of the proletariat to a relative fringe of radical minorities, including (in the United States) the student New Left and militant groups such as the Black Panther Party.

Critical theorists initially believed that they could liberate people from false beliefs, or "false consciousness," and in particular from ideologies that served to maintain the political and economic status quo, by pointing out to them that they had acquired these beliefs in irrational ways (e.g., through indoctrination). In the end, however, some theorists, notably Marcuse, wondered whether the forces tending to promote ideological conformity in modern capitalist societies had so compromised the perceptions and reasoning powers of most individuals that no rational critique would ever be effective.

## JÜRGEN HABERMAS

In works published from the 1960s, the German philosopher Jürgen Habermas attempted to expand the scope of critical theory by incorporating ideas from contemporary analytic philosophy, in particular the speech act theory developed by J.L. Austin and his student John Searle. Habermas argued that human beings have a fundamental interest in coming to agreement with each other in open rational dialogue. He also held that, in ordinary speech situations, people commit themselves to the truth of the assertions they make; in particular, they implicitly claim that their assertions can be vindicated in an "ideal speech situation"—a dialogue that is completely free and uncoerced, in which no force prevails but that of the better argument.

The notion of an ideal speech situation suggests a certain approach to politics as well. Assuming that "correct" political values and goals are those that everyone would agree to in an ideal speech situation, a political process that produces policies or laws on the basis of forms of communication that are less than ideal (i.e., rationally distorted) is to that extent suspect. The ideal of "deliberative democracy" is thus implicit in Habermas's ethical analysis of communication ("communicative ethics"), and his own writings explicitly elaborate this point. According to this view, the aim of democratic politics should be to generate a conversation that leads to a rational consensus about the common good. Of course, the ideal by itself does not determine what particular laws or constitutional arrangements ought to exist in any specific society. In this sense, communicative ethics is formal and procedural rather than substantive. Philosophy can define the moral point of view, but it cannot dictate or predict what rational persons would agree to in an ideal discussion aimed at truth.

## LOGICAL-POSITIVIST INTERLUDE

Political and ethical philosophy in English-speaking countries in the first half of the 20th century was inhibited to some extent by the advent in the early 1930s of logical positivism, which conceived of knowledge claims on the model of the hypotheses of natural science. According to the simplest version of logical positivism, genuine knowledge claims can be divided into two groups: (1) those that can be verified or falsified on the basis of observation, or sense experience (empirical claims); and (2) those that are true or false simply by virtue of the conventional meanings assigned to the words they contain (tautologies or contradictions), along with their logical implications. All other claims, including the evaluative assertions made by traditional political and ethical philosophers, are literally meaningless, hence not worth discussing. A complementary view held by some logical positivists was that an evaluative assertion, properly understood, is not a statement of fact but either an expression of the speaker's attitude (e.g., of approval or disapproval) or an imperative—a speech act aimed at influencing the behaviour of others. This view of the language of ethical and political philosophy tended to limit serious study in those fields until the 1960s, when logical positivism came to be regarded as simplistic in its conceptions of linguistic meaning and scientific practice.

# THE PHILOSOPHICAL LIBERALISM OF JOHN RAWLS

The publication of *A Theory of Justice* (1971), by the American philosopher John Rawls, spurred a revival of interest in the philosophical foundations of political liberalism. The viability of liberalism was thereafter a major theme of political philosophy in English-speaking countries.

According to the American philosopher Thomas Nagel, liberalism is the conjunction of two ideals: (1) individuals should have liberty of thought and speech and wide freedom to live their lives as they choose (so long as they do not harm others in certain ways), and (2) individuals in any society should be able to determine through majority rule the laws by which they are governed and should not be so unequal in status or wealth that they have unequal opportunities to participate in democratic decision making. Various traditional and modern versions of liberalism differ from each other in their interpretation of these ideals and in the relative importance they assign to them.

In *A Theory of Justice*, Rawls observed that a necessary condition of justice in any society is that each individual should be the equal bearer of certain rights that cannot be disregarded under any circumstances, even if doing so would advance the general welfare or satisfy the demands of a majority. This condition cannot be met by utilitarianism, because that ethical theory would countenance forms of government in which the greater happiness of a majority is achieved by neglecting the rights and interests of a minority. Hence, utilitarianism is unsatisfactory as a theory of justice, and another theory must be sought.

*Harvard political philosopher John Rawls.* Steve Pyke/Premium Archive/Getty Images

According to Rawls, a just society is one whose major political, social, and economic institutions, taken together, satisfy the following two principles:

1. Each person has an equal claim to a scheme of basic rights and liberties that is the maximum consistent with the same scheme for all.

2. Social and economic inequalities are permissible only if: (a) they confer the greatest benefit to the least-advantaged members of society, and (b) they are attached to positions and offices open to all under conditions of fair equality of opportunity.

The basic rights and liberties in principle 1 include the rights and liberties of democratic citizenship, such as the right to vote; the right to run for office in free elections; freedom of speech, assembly, and religion; the right to a fair trial; and, more generally, the right to the rule of law. Principle 1 is accorded strict priority over principle 2, which regulates social and economic inequalities.

Principle 2 combines two ideals. The first, known as the "difference principle," requires that any unequal distribution of social or economic goods (e.g., wealth) must be such that the least-advantaged members of society would be better off under that distribution than they would be under any other distribution consistent with principle 1, including an equal distribution. (A slightly unequal distribution might benefit the least advantaged by encouraging greater overall productivity.) The second ideal is meritocracy, understood in a very demanding way. According to Rawls, fair equality of opportunity obtains in a society when all persons with the same native talent (genetic inheritance) and the same degree of ambition have the same prospects for success in all competitions for positions that confer special economic and social advantages.

Why suppose with Rawls that justice requires an approximately egalitarian redistribution of social and economic goods? After all, a person who prospers in a market economy might plausibly say, "I earned my wealth. Therefore, I am entitled to keep it." But how one fares in a market economy depends on luck as well as effort. There is the luck of being in the right place at the right time and of benefiting from unpredictable shifts in supply and demand, but there is also the luck of being born with greater or lesser intelligence and other desirable traits, along with the luck of growing up in a nurturing environment. No one can take credit for this kind of luck, but it decisively influences how one fares in the many competitions by which social and economic goods are distributed. Indeed, sheer brute luck is so thoroughly intermixed with the contributions one makes to one's own success (or failure) that it is ultimately impossible to distinguish what a person is responsible for from what he is not. Given this fact, Rawls urges, the only plausible justification of inequality is that it serves to render everyone better off, especially those who have the least.

Rawls tries to accommodate his theory of justice to what he takes to be the important fact that reasonable people disagree deeply about the nature of morality and the good life and will continue to do so in any nontyrannical society that respects freedom of speech. He aims to render his theory noncommittal on these controversial matters and to posit a set of principles of justice that all reasonable persons can accept as valid, despite their disagreements.

# LIBERTARIANISM

Despite its wide appeal, Rawls's liberal egalitarianism soon faced challengers. An early conservative rival was libertarianism, sometimes called "classical liberalism" for its similarity to the views of early liberals such as John Locke.

## LIBERTARIAN PHILOSOPHY

According to libertarianism, because each person is literally the sole rightful owner of himself, no one has property rights in anyone else (no person can own another person), and no one owes anything to anyone else. By "appropriating" unowned things, an individual may acquire over them full private ownership rights, which he may give away or exchange. One has the right to do whatever one chooses with whatever one legitimately owns, as long as one does not harm others in specified ways—i.e., by coercion, force, violence, fraud, theft, extortion, or physical damage to another's property. According to libertarians, Rawlsian liberal egalitarianism is unjust because it would allow (indeed, require) the state to redistribute social and economic goods without their owners' consent, in violation of their private ownership rights.

The most spirited and sophisticated presentation of the libertarian critique was *Anarchy, State, and Utopia* (1974), by the American philosopher Robert Nozick (1938–2002). Nozick also argued that a "minimal state," one that limited its activities to the enforcement of people's basic libertarian rights, could have arisen in a hypothetical "state of nature" through a process in which no one's basic libertarian rights are violated. He regarded this demonstration as a refutation of anarchism, the doctrine that the state is inherently unjustified.

# CONTEMPORARY LIBERTARIANISM

In the second half of the 20th century, explicitly libertarian political parties (such as the Libertarian Party in the United States and the Libertarianz Party in New Zealand) garnered little support, even among self-professed libertarians. Most politically active libertarians supported classical liberal parties (such as the Free Democratic Party in Germany or the Flemish Liberals and Democrats in Belgium) or conservative parties (such as the Republican Party in the United States or the Conservative Party in Great Britain); they also backed pressure groups advocating policies such as tax reduction, the privatization of education, and the decriminalization of drugs and other so-called victimless crimes. There were also small but vocal groups of libertarians in Scandinavia, Latin America, India, and China. In the early 21st century the economic policies of the Republican Party increasingly reflected libertarian priorities. Starting in 2009 the libertarian-inspired Tea Party movement in the United States cultivated popular animus toward the federal government while promoting policies such as tax reduction and opposition to federal programs and regulations designed to increase the availability of health insurance.

The publication of Nozick's *Anarchy, State, and Utopia* marked the beginning of an intellectual revival of libertarianism. Libertarian ideas in economics became increasingly influential as libertarian economists were appointed to prominent advisory positions in conservative governments in the United Kingdom and the United States and as some libertarians, such as James M. Buchanan, Milton Friedman, F.A. Hayek, and Vernon L. Smith, were awarded the Nobel Prize for Economics. In 1982 the death of the libertarian novelist and social theorist Ayn Rand prompted a surge of popular interest in her work. Libertarian scholars, activists, and political leaders also played prominent roles in the worldwide

Tea Party protestors demonstrate outside the University of Michigan in 2010. The Tea Party movement in the United States is influenced by contemporary libertarianism. Bill Pugliano/ Getty Images

campaign against apartheid and in the construction of democratic societies in eastern and central Europe following the collapse of communism there in 1989–1991. In the early 21st century, libertarian ideas informed new research in diverse fields such as history, law, economic development, telecommunications, bioethics, globalization, and social theory.

## AYN RAND

(b. Feb. 2, 1905, St. Petersburg, Russia—
d. March 6, 1982, New York, N.Y., U.S.)

Ayn Rand was a Russian-born American writer who, in commercially successful novels, presented her philosophy of objectivism, essentially reversing the traditional Judeo-Christian ethic.

Rand graduated from the University of Petrograd in 1924 and two years later immigrated to the United States. She initially worked as a screenwriter in Hollywood and in 1931 became a naturalized U.S. citizen. Her first novel, *We, the Living*, was published in 1936. *The Fountainhead* (1943), her first best-selling novel, depicts a highly romanticized architect-hero, a superior individual whose egoism and genius prevail over timid traditionalism and social conformism. The allegorical *Atlas Shrugged* (1957), another best-seller, combines science fiction and political allegory in telling of an anticollectivist strike called by the management of U.S. big industry, a company of attractive, self-made men.

The doctrine of objectivism shaped Rand's work. A deeply conservative view, it posited individual effort and ability as the sole source of all genuine achievement, thereby elevating the pursuit of self-interest to the role of first principle and scorning such notions as altruism and sacrifice for the common good as liberal delusions and even vices. It further held laissez-faire capitalism to be most congenial to the exercise of talent. Rand's objectivism underlay her fiction but found more direct expression in her nonfiction, including such works as *For the New Intellectual* (1961), *The Virtue of Selfishness* (1965), *Capitalism: The Unknown Ideal* (1966), *Introduction to Objectivist Epistemology* (1967), and *Philosophy: Who Needs It?* (1982). She also promoted objectivism in the journals *The Objectivist* (1962–1971) and *The Ayn Rand Letter* (1971–1976).

Rand's controversial views attracted a faithful audience of admirers and followers, many of whom first encountered her novels as teenagers. Although her work influenced generations of conservative politicians and government officials in the United States, it was not well regarded among academic philosophers, most of whom dismissed it as shallow. She was working on an adaptation of *Atlas Shrugged* for a television miniseries when she died.

# COMMUNITARIANISM

In the 1980s adherents of communitarianism, such as Michael Sandel and Michael Walzer, argued for the importance of the common good in opposition to contemporary liberals and libertarians, who emphasized the good for individuals, particularly including personal autonomy and individual rights. In 1990 the political theorists Amitai Etzioni and William Galston founded a school known as "responsive" communitarianism—the main thesis of which was that people face two major sources of normativity, that of the common good and that of autonomy and rights, neither of which in principle should take precedence over the other. Their ideas were eventually elaborated in academic and popular books and periodicals, gaining thereby a measure of political currency, mainly in the West.

A central theme of communitarianism is the close relation between the individual and the community. Sandel and Taylor, among other academic communitarians, held that contemporary liberalism and libertarianism presuppose an incoherent notion of the individual as existing outside and apart from society rather than embedded within it. To the contrary, they argued, there are no generic individuals but rather only Germans or Russians, Berliners or Muscovites, or members of some other particularistic community. Because individual identity is partly constituted (or "constructed") by culture and social relations, there is no coherent way of formulating individual rights or interests in abstraction from social contexts. In particular, according to these communitarians, there is no point in attempting to found a theory of justice on principles that individuals would choose in a hypothetical state of ignorance of their social, economic, and historical circumstances (from behind a Rawlsian "veil of ignorance"), because such individuals cannot exist, even in principle.

Communitarians also drew upon Aristotle and Hegel to argue that some conception of the good must be formulated on the social level and that the community cannot be a normative-neutral realm. Unless there is a social formulation of the good, there can be no normative foundation upon which to draw to settle conflicts of value between different individuals and groups. Such an overriding good (e.g., the national well-being) enables persons with different moral outlooks or ideological backgrounds to find principled (rather than merely prudential) common ground.

## MICHEL FOUCAULT AND POSTMODERNISM

The work of the French philosopher and historian Michel Foucault (1926–1984) has implications for political philosophy even though it does not directly address the traditional issues of the field. Much of Foucault's writing is not so much philosophy as it is philosophically informed intellectual history. *Naissance de la clinique: une archéologie du regard médical* (1963; *The Birth of the Clinic: An Archaeology of Medical Perception*), for example, examines the notion of illness and the beginnings of modern medicine in the late 18th and early 19th centuries, and *Surveiller et punir: naissance de la prison* (1975; *Discipline and Punish: The Birth of the Prison*) studies the origins of the practice of punishing criminals by imprisonment.

One of Foucault's aims was to undermine the notion that the emergence of modern political liberalism and its characteristic institutions (e.g., individual rights and representative democracy) in the late 18th century resulted in greater freedom for the individual. He argued to the contrary that modern liberal societies are oppressive, though the oppressive practices they employ are not as overt as in earlier times. Modern forms of oppression tend to be hard to recognize as such, because they are justified by ostensibly objective and impartial branches of social science. In a process that Foucault called "normalization," a supposedly objective social science labels as "normal" or "rational" behaviour that society deems respectable or desirable, so behaviour deemed otherwise becomes abnormal or irrational and a legitimate object of discipline or coercion. Behaviour that is perceived as odd, for example, may be classified as a symptom of mental illness. Foucault viewed modern bureaucratic institutions as exuding a spirit of rationality, scientific expertise, and humane concern but as really amounting to an arbitrary exercise of power by one group over another.

Foucault advocated resistance to the political status quo and the power of established institutions. But he was skeptical of any attempt to argue that one political regime or set of practices is morally superior to another. The use of rational argument to support or oppose a political view, according to Foucault, is merely another attempt to exercise arbitrary power over others. Accordingly, he eschewed any blueprint for political reform or any explicit articulation of moral or rational norms that society ought to uphold. In a 1983 interview he summarized his political attitude in these words:

> *My point is not that everything is bad, but that everything is dangerous, which is not exactly the same as bad. If everything is dangerous, then we always have something to do. So my position leads not to apathy but to a hyper- and pessimistic activism.*

Foucault's ideas gave rise in the 1970s and '80s to philosophical postmodernism, a movement characterized by broad epistemological skepticism and ethical subjectivism, a general suspicion of reason, and an acute sensitivity to the role of ideology in asserting and maintaining political and economic power. Postmodernists attacked the attempt by Enlightenment philosophers and others to discover allegedly objective moral values that could serve as a standard for assessing different political systems or for measuring political progress from one historical period to another. According to Jean-François Lyotard (1924–1998), for example, this project represents a secular faith that must be abandoned. In *La Condition postmoderne* (1979; *The Postmodern Condition*) and other writings, Lyotard declared his suspicion of what he called "grand narratives"—putatively rational, overarching accounts, such as Marxism and liberalism, of how the world is or ought to be. He asserted that political conflicts in contemporary societies reflect the clash of incommensurable values and perspectives and are therefore not rationally decidable.

## FEMINIST SOCIAL AND POLITICAL PHILOSOPHY

The earliest feminist philosophers examined gender bias in traditional social and political institutions. By asking the question "Who benefits?" they showed how mostly unspoken practices of gender-based exclusion and discrimination favoured the interests of men. Much of their analysis concerned sexual and family relations, which were then considered private or personal matters that could not (or should not) be addressed by political means. Accordingly, with a fine disregard, they adopted the rallying cry "The personal is political."

The traditional political philosophies of liberalism and Marxism generally ignored sexual and family issues; in contrast, feminist philosophers made them the focus of political theory. Eventually three major schools of feminist political theory arose, each emphasizing a distinctive subset of issues: liberal feminism, socialist feminism, and radical feminism.

Liberal feminists—e.g., Susan Moller Okin—pointed out the many ways in which gender discrimination defeats women's aspirations, and they defended reforms designed to make women's equality a social and political reality. Noting that differences in the ways in which girls and boys are raised served to channel women and men into different and unequal social roles, they advocated gender-neutral forms of education and child rearing. They particularly focused on protecting and extending the rights that enabled women to pursue self-chosen goals, such as reproductive rights (including the right to legally obtain an abortion) and rights to full educational and economic opportunities.

Whereas liberal feminists applied the core liberal values of freedom and equality to address women's concerns, the socialist feminists Alison Jaggar and Iris Marion Young appropriated Marxist categories, which were based on labour and economic structures. Criticizing traditional Marxism for exaggerating the importance of waged labour outside the home, socialist feminists insisted that the unpaid caregiving and homemaking that women are expected to perform are equally indispensable forms of labour and that the sexual division of labour that assigns most domestic work to women is exploitative. They also objected to the double day of work that burdens most women who have children and who work outside the home. Likewise, they condemned the economic dependency and insecurity of stay-at-home mothers and the low salaries of child-care workers.

Lastly, the school of radical feminism turned women's attention to sexuality and to the disparities of power that pervade heterosexual relationships in patriarchal cultures. According to radical feminists, male heterosexuality objectifies the female body and makes the domination and degradation of women a source of erotic stimulation. Such assertions were the basis of Catharine MacKinnon's and Andrea Dworkin's campaigns in the 1980s and '90s against

Tens of thousands of women participating in the World March of Women in Bukavu, Democratic Republic of Congo, on October 17, 2010. Women from 43 nations took part in this particular march. AFP/Getty Images

sexual harassment and pornography. Likewise, those assertions provided the basis of Marilyn Frye's endorsement of separatist feminist practices.

Liberal, socialist, and radical feminism continue to challenge standard philosophical assumptions about the scope of politics and the nature of justice. Yet, arguably, each of them rests on a flawed conception of gender. As Elizabeth V. Spelman, María Lugones, and Judith Butler claimed, none adequately takes into account the ways in which gender is influenced by and interacts with sexual orientation, race, ethnicity, class, age, and ability, and none explicitly addresses how those factors affect the needs of diverse groups of women. Moreover, as Uma Narayan argued, none comes to grips with the complexities of advancing women's rights internationally or with the obstacles to coordinating feminist agendas in a globalized economy.

Much current work in feminist social and political philosophy—specifically in black feminist theory, queer theory, and feminist human rights theory—takes on these urgent problems.

## TWENTY-FIRST–CENTURY QUESTIONS

The history of Western political philosophy from Plato to the present day makes plain that the discipline is still faced with the basic problems defined by the Greeks. The need to redeploy public power in order to maintain the survival and enhance the quality of human life, for example, has never been so essential. And, if the opportunities for promoting well-being are now far greater, the penalties for the abuse of power are nothing less than the destruction of most forms of life on the planet, whether through war or environmental catastrophe or both.

From another perspective, however, the political problems of the present day are interestingly unique, giving rise to theoretical questions that earlier political philosophers did not have to confront. Two contrasting features of the world in the early 21st century, for example, are the increasing integration of national political and economic systems and the continuing gross inequality of wealth between developed and less-developed, or underdeveloped, countries. Both features suggest the desirability, even the necessity, of developing political philosophy in order to make it more applicable in a global context. Such considerations have led the Indian economist Amartya Sen and the American philosopher Martha Nussbaum to explore the possibility of a "global" theory of justice.

Nussbaum has argued that every inhabitant of the globe is entitled to the conditions that enable one to attain a decent and objectively worthwhile and valuable quality of life. Other philosophers have argued for the justice or

*Nobel Laureate and economist Amartya Sen addressing the crowd during the inauguration of the Fifth Annual Global Development Network conference in New Delhi, India, on January 27, 2004.*
Prakash Singh/AFP/Getty Images

necessity of a single world government or of forms of government other than the nation-state.

The advent of nuclear weapons in the mid-20th century increased interest in traditional just-war theory, especially as it applies to the issue of the proportionate use of force. Later in the century, the proliferation not only of nuclear but also of chemical and biological weapons made the application of just-war theory to the contemporary scene seem all the more urgent. In the view of some thinkers, the increasing menace of international terrorism in the early 21st century — horrifically illustrated by the 2001 September 11 attacks in the United States — has changed the scope and conditions of justly prosecuted wars, though others vehemently disagree. Following the U.S.-led invasion of Iraq in 2003, some scholars argued that the war had failed to meet some traditional conditions on the just use of force, including that there be a "just cause" (e.g., self-defense against imminent attack), that force be used only as a last resort, and that the force be proportionate to the threat. The nature of terrorism has itself become a philosophically debated question, some philosophers going so far as to assert that in some real-world circumstances terrorism may be justified.

The adoption by many countries of liberal-democratic forms of government in the second half of the 20th century, especially after the fall of Soviet and eastern European communism in 1989–1991, led some political theorists to speculate that the liberal model of government has been vindicated by history or even (as American writer and political theorist, Francis Fukuyama [1952- ] asserted) that it represents the "end" of history—the culmination of the millennia-long political development of humankind. Be that as it may, many theorists, confident of the basic viability of liberalism, have taken the view that the most important questions of political theory have been settled in liberalism's favour, and all that remains is to work out the details.

Others are not so convinced. One issue that continues to be troublesome for liberalism is its traditional posture of benevolent neutrality toward religion. Some liberal theorists have proposed that this posture should be extended to all disputed questions concerning what constitutes a good life. Yet millions of people around the world, even in the West, continue to reject the separation of church and state, and millions of others have objected to state policies that allow the pursuit of conceptions of the good life with which they disagree. In these respects, liberalism may be out of sync (rightly or wrongly) with the political aspirations of much of the world's population.

All this suggests a rather homely conclusion: the future direction of political philosophy, like that of political practice, is uncertain. If anything is likely, it is that there will be much for political philosophers to think about.

# CONCLUSION

As the reader will well appreciate by this point, the two approaches to the study of politics explored in this book, despite their fundamental differences, are not in conflict with each other. Political science and political philosophy are not competitors, and indeed the modern history of the two disciplines shows that they frequently complement and inform each other. Political philosophy would be unrealistic and doomed to irrelevance if it were to ignore completely the brute facts of political and social life as revealed by the social sciences, especially political science. Fortunately, this has not been the case, and in fact some relatively recent theoretical developments, such as feminist critiques of traditional political philosophy and communitarian critiques of philosophical liberalism, have relied upon new research in political science, socioeconomics, law, and social and developmental psychology, among other disciplines. Likewise, research in political science is generally not conducted in a moral vacuum but at a fundamental level reflects assumptions about the larger purposes the discipline should serve (if only in the long run) or about the values it should respect. This fact is most vividly illustrated in the fields of political culture and democratic theory, both of which presuppose that democracy is a good thing, that democracy is good in part because of the individual rights and liberties it guarantees, and that one of the goals of research should be to contribute (albeit indirectly) to the spread of democracy by identifying the factors that help to strengthen or undermine democratic forms of government. At a more basic level, philosophical theorizing has informed some of the traditional categories and assumptions of political science, including the notion of the political itself, the nature of the state, the relations between the state and civil society, the distinction between the public and the private realms, the nature of political authority, the shifting content of individual rights, the conditions of political autonomy and freedom of choice, the notion of the perfectibility of society, and, perhaps most fundamental of all, the ideas of human development and the human good.

In truth, politics cannot be adequately understood without appreciating the contributions of both political science and political philosophy. The purpose of this book has been to present the subject of politics from both of these complementary and essential perspectives.

# Glossary

**aristocracy** A government in which power is vested in a minority consisting of those believed to be best qualified.

**autocracy** Government in which one person possesses unlimited power.

**behaviourism** A school of psychology that takes the objective evidence of behaviour (conceived as responses to stimuli) to be the only legitimate concern of pscyhological research and regards conscious experience as irrelevant.

**bureaucracy** Specific form of organization characterized by complexity, division of labour, permanence, professional management, hierarchical coordination and control, a strict chain of command, and legal authority.

**demagogue** A leader who makes use of popular prejudices and false claims and promises in order to gain power.

**democracy** A government in which the supreme power is vested in the people and exercised by them directly or indirectly through a system of representation, usually involving periodically held free elections.

**empirical** Originating in or based on observation or experience.

**epistemological** Of or relating to the theory of the nature and grounds of knowledge especially with reference to its limits and validity.

**humanism** A philosophy that usually rejects supernaturalism and stresses an individual's dignity and worth and capacity for self-realization through reason.

**kulak** A prosperous or wealthy peasant farmer in 19th-century Russia.

**liberalism** Political doctrine that takes protecting and enhancing the freedom of the individual to be the central problem of politics.

**monarchy** A government having a hereditary chief of state with life tenure and powers varying from nominal to absolute.

**normative** Of, relating to, or determining norms or standards.

**objectivism** Philosophical system identified with the thought of the 20th-century Russian-born American writer Ayn Rand.

**polity** A form of political organization described by Aristotle in which rich and poor respect each other's rights and the best-qualified citizens rule with the consent of all.

**positivism** Any system that confines itself to the data of experience and excludes a priori or metaphysical speculations.

**proletariat** The class of industrial workers who lack their own means of production and hence sell their labour to live.

**rational choice theory** The school of thought that holds that political behaviour is best understood as a rational pursuit of self-interest on the part of the actors involved.

**Stoicism** A school of thought that flourished in Greek and Roman antiquity that urged participation in human affairs and emphasized a mode of conduct characterized by tranquillity of mind and certainty of moral worth.

**structuralism** In political science, the view that all political choices take place within specific institutional structures.

**totalitarianism** Form of government in which the citizen is totally subject to an absolute state authority.

## POLITICAL SCIENCE

There are few modern classics of political science, but among those considered indispensable are Joseph Schumpeter, *Capitalism, Socialism and Democracy*, 6th ed. (1987); E.E. Schattschneider, *The Semisovereign People: A Realist's View of Democracy in America* (1960, reissued 1988); and V.O. Key, *Politics, Parties and Pressure Groups*, 5th ed. (1964), and *The Responsible Electorate* (1966, reissued 1968). Modern political theory, including rational choice theory, owes much to Mancur Olson, *The Logic of Collective Action: Public Goods and the Theory of Groups* (1968, reissued 1995). Samuel P. Huntington has been a major force in post-World War II political science, especially his *Political Order in Changing Societies* (1968) and *The Clash of Civilizations and the Remaking of World Order* (1996). Robert A. Dahl, *Modern Political Analysis*, 5th ed. (1991), is an excellent guide to the renowned political scientist's views. Seymour Martin Lipset, *Political Man: The Social Bases of Politics* (1960), is a prime example of the behavioral approach, and his *American Exceptionalism: A Double-Edged Sword* (1996) illustrates the historical-cultural approach. The historical-cultural perspective is also the focus of Robert Putnam, *Making Democracy Work: Civic Traditions in Modern Italy* (1993), and *Bowling Alone: The Collapse and Revival of American Community* (2001).

# POLITICAL PHILOSOPHY

Accessible general discussions are Jonathan Wolff, *An Introduction to Political Philosophy,* 2nd rev. ed. (2006); and Will Kymlicka, *Contemporary Political Philosophy: An Introduction,* 2nd ed. (2002). The Cambridge anthologies bring together scholarly articles on most of the major periods: C.J. Rowe and Malcolm Schofield (eds.), *The Cambridge History of Greek and Roman Political Thought* (2000); J.H. Burns (ed.), *The Cambridge History of Medieval Political Thought c. 350–1450* (1988); J.H. Burns and Mark Goldie (eds.), *The Cambridge History of Political Thought: 1450–1700* (1991); and Terence Ball and Richard Bellamy (eds.), *The Cambridge History of Twentieth-Century Political Thought* (2003). The modern period is treated in Iain Hampsher-Monk, *A History of Modern Political Thought: Major Political Thinkers from Hobbes to Marx* (1992).

Each person has an equal claim to a scheme of basic rights and liberties that is the maximum consistent with the same scheme for all.

Social and economic inequalities are permissible only if: (a) they confer the greatest benefit to the least-advantaged members of society, and (b) they are attached to positions and offices open to all under conditions of fair equality of opportunity.

# Index